SOUTHERN PORTUGAL

Its people, traditions and wildlife

SOUTHERN PORTUGAL

Its people, traditions and wildlife

John and Madge Measures

First published in 1995 by
Associação "In Loco"
Apartado 603
8000 Faro
Portugal

ISBN 972 8262 00 0

Edited and designed by
D & N Publishing
Crowood Lane, Ramsbury
Marlborough, Wiltshire SN8 2HR

Editor: Donald Greig
Maps: Zea Martins

Colour separation by Fotographics Ltd,
London–Hong Kong.
Printed and bound in Hong Kong.

DEDICATION

This book is dedicated to all the inhabitants of the Caldeirão region, without whom the book would never have been conceived.

ACKNOWLEDGEMENTS

During our research for this book we have travelled many thousands of kilometres and met many hundreds of people to whom we would like to extend our grateful thanks for their undaunting help: artisans, agriculturalists, naturalists and many other specialists whose names are too numerous to mention.

In particular we must thank the following: all the staff of IN LOCO in Faro; the presidents and officials of the *concelhos* and *freguesias*; Carlos Rosa and his wife Joanna in Almodôvar; the ladies in the *Turismo* of Mértola, Lagos and Alcoutim; Christine Tucker, Production Assistant BBC Open University, Milton Keynes, for the excellent video *The Hidden Algarve*; Frank Murray for developing the films in record time; Zea for all the maps; and Senhor Horta of the Avenida Restaurant in Mértola for his introductions and general information.

Once again, David Price-Goodfellow of D & N Publishing has given advice and help and we are greatly indebted to him.

Above all, we must thank Dr Alberto Melo who made all this possible.

CONTENTS

FOREWORD

As the dominant, worldwide model of economic growth grew and accelerated its pace in recent decades, most rural areas were overcome by the trend to concentrate resources, people and capital in a few selected urbanized or industrialized sites. The consequent impact was felt in two opposing directions, generally depending on the relative distances of each rural area to an important focus of economical and financial investment. Such areas were thus either 're-adjusted', incorporated within the new urban-industrial environment, or left aside and gradually depleted of their main human resources and capacities. Despite the apparent contrast, both assimilation and depletion lead to the same fate: the impending extinction of genuine rural areas in Europe and elsewhere.

However, rural life needs to survive and develop, but not in isolation or as a nostalgic memorial. Our psychological welfare as well as our quality of life, cultural diversity and creativeness, not to mention the ecological balance, all require the maintenance within our societies of rural areas. There is no doubt that these 'isles of irrationality' now face an increasing threat of extinction, with the wide range of human, social, economic, cultural and environmental effects involved. Nevertheless they can also be seen as strongholds of resistance against the steam-rolling trend of cultural homogeneity and product standardization. Contemporary politics and economics have to tackle the crucial problem by the end of the century: how to tally the revenue increasingly generated by the modernized urban-industrial system (which is merely aggravating existing surpluses) with the wealth which is lost when villages are deserted, cultures and skills are forgotten, fields are abandoned, and landscapes ruined.

The sierra between Algarve and Alentejo in southern Portugal is just one of many European rural areas now facing a slow death. There is so much wealth there, but so little revenue to maintain local families and guarantee reasonable living standards in today's world.

This book is precisely about such wealth, the hidden assets and resources of an 'invisible' vast area which never appears in the glossy tourist brochures that have transformed the Algarve into – and maintain as – one of the most popular resorts for mass tourism.

Only 20 miles from the cosmopolitan coast of the Algarve lies an extremely rich and varied world where nature, culture and history lie waiting to be discovered by the discerning visitor willing to explore one of the last outposts of rural Europe.

And who could be better guides to the southernmost hills and villages of Portugal than John and Madge Measures, who have lived for over 25 years in this extremity of our continent and have regularly – and lovingly – visited all localities, learning from the people and appreciating the scenery. This book is written from the heart as well as from the mind, and we wish all our readers a similar experience of personal fulfilment when exploring the many roads, valleys, streams, hills, hamlets and villages of the mystery-laden *Serra do Caldeirão* (also known as 'Mu'). Thanks to the authors, these mountains will now become less mysterious, but even more magical.

Opposite Typical scenery on the sand dunes near the west coast.

Professor Alberto Melo
Chairman, IN *LOCO* Association

7

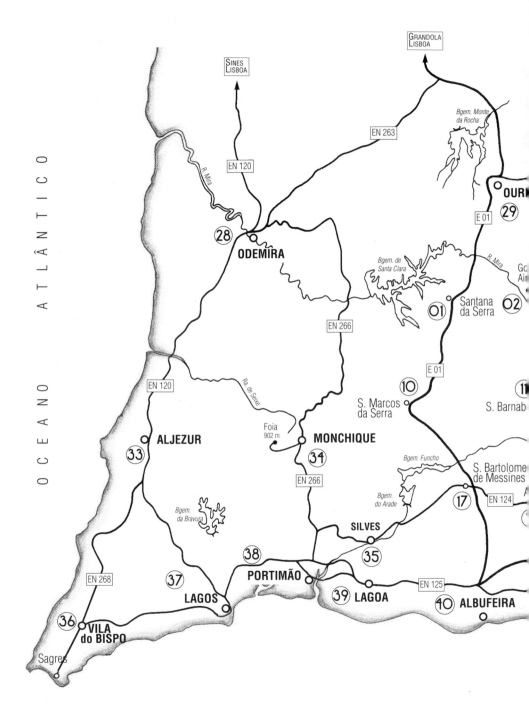

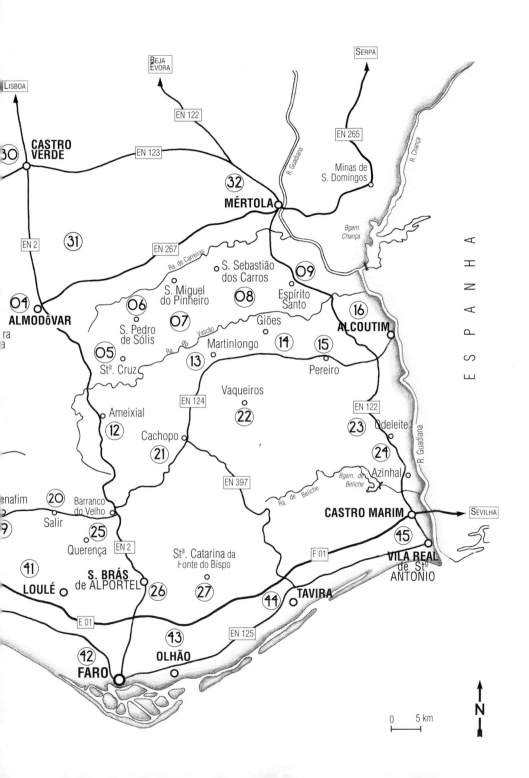

SECTION 1
INTRODUCTION

LANDFORM

Mainland Portugal (excluding Madeira and the Azores) covers an area of 88,226 sq km. This book covers approximately one eighth of this, lying between latitudes 38.00 and 36.58N, and longitudes 7.25 and 9.00W. The imaginary boundary line runs from Odemira in the west through Ourique, Castro Verde, Mértola and on to the Rio Chança in the east and therefore includes part of the Baixo Alentejo and all of the Algarve.

The geology of southern Portugal is complex. The southern littoral is a sedimentary layer composed of gravel, sandstone and alluvium. The soil is rich, as can be seen in the deep red loam and good crops near the coastline, where there is adequate water for irrigation. Further to the north is the *barrocal*, a lens-shaped area of limestone stretching from the high 100m dolomitic cliffs at Cabo de São Vicente, widening out in the centre of the Algarve north-east of Faro, and ending east of Loulé. This limestone is mainly hard dolomitic and is used for producing *cal*, a burnt lime.

To the north, stretching into the Alentejo, is a high area of Carboniferous slate which is hard and impervious but is easily split by tree roots. A contact zone of

The open-cast mine at São Domingos. At the beginning of the century it was one of the largest mines producing copper and sulphur in Europe. It finally closed in 1965, but in recent years a continuation of this mineral vein has been exploited underground at Neves Corvo on the Almodôvar and Castro Verde border.

Triassic sandstone occurs where the lime-stone meets the Carboniferous slate. This line varies in width from about 1km to 3km or more near Silves. Along this zone lie most of the major towns and villages within the interior of the Algarve. Important mineral veins come to the surface, mainly copper and tin at Neves Corvo and copper and sul-phur at the now abandoned Mina de São Domingos. The Serra de Monchique, rising to 902m, is composed of syenite. The form found here is a hard, fine-grained variety called monchiquite, which is quarried just south of Monchique town.

HISTORICAL BACKGROUND

Portugal's historic past is extremely rich, but generally unexploited. Many archaeo-logical sites within southern Portugal are still being excavated, but this is a long and arduous process and, because of the expense involved, many of these digs are simply summer occupations for students with expert archaeologists in attendance.

Within the area covered by this book, history appears to begin with the Bronze

Castro da Cola. This shows all that remains of the Arabic castle and fortress which played an important role from the 8th to 13th centuries, before finally being abandoned in the 14th. This is one of many sites on an archaeological circuit which includes Neolithic tombs and has a directional plan *in situ* near the church.

and Copper Ages, which occurred between 3000 and 1000 BC and are represented by burial sites near Santana da Serra (no. 01) on the Circuit da Cola and dolmen burial chambers at Alcalar near Portimão (38). Evidence of the pre-Roman era between 500 BC and AD 150 is also apparent, in the Mesas dos Castelinhos at Santa-Clara-a-Nova (03) in the southern Alentejo, while the Roman times are manifested by the 3rd-century bridge in Almodôvar (04) and the Roman forum and cryptoporticum in the museum town of Mértola (32) .

The Arabs invaded this area during the 8th century and many monuments are credited to their 500-year domination, which culminated in their local overthrow by Afonso Henriques in 1139 at the Battle of Ourique, followed by their final expulsion from Faro (42) in 1249. Aljezur (33), Ourique (29), Castro Verde (30), Almodôvar (04), Mértola (32), Faro, Silves (35) and many more locations throughout the region testify to the occupation, with many sites in an extremely good state of repair.

On 16 June 1373 the first Treaty of Alliance was signed in London. This treaty

The Roman bridge over the Ribeira de Cobres was renovated in the 1970s and can clearly be seen from the newer road bridge on the southern entrance to Almodôvar on the EN2 road from the Algarve. In its heyday it was on the important Via III which went from Salacia (Setúbal) to Ossonoba (Faro).

The Prison Hatch in Almodôvar city museum. This fascinating museum with walls 150cm thick was once a palace and also a prison. Almodôvar is a historically rich town well worth exploring. On its western outskirts the ruins of a medieval manor house give an insight into the lifestyle of a bygone age.

is still in effect today, thus making Portugal England's oldest ally.

In 1703 the Methuen Treaty facilitated the export of wool from England to Oporto in exchange for port, thus starting a long association with the Douro valley.

In the 15th century, Portugal was at the height of its maritime power, with Prince Henry the Navigator sending out his ships' captain Gil Eanes and other experienced navigators to find a route down the coast of Africa, eventually to open the way to India. Diogo Cão reached the Congo in 1482 and Bartolomeu Dias rounded the Cape of Good Hope in 1488, while Pedro Alvares Cabral discovered Brazil in 1500.

From 1149, except for the period from 1580 to 1 December 1640 when Spain was in power, Portugal remained a kingdom (in earlier times described as Portugal and the Algarve) until the overthrow of the monarchy in 1910, when it became a republic. The bloodless revolution in 1974 ousted the then ruling dictatorship, opening the way for the country to develop a democratic constitution.

ARCHITECTURE

The Late Gothic architectural style spread throughout Europe between 1250 and 1500, while Manueline was prevalent in Portugal for a short period between 1490 and 1540. There are some good examples of Manueline architecture within this area, but a vast number of the houses, churches, cathedrals and castles were severely damaged or destroyed during the earthquake of 1 November 1755. Therefore, most of the monuments and churches were built after this time. This extravagant and unique style took root during the reign of Dom Manuel (1495–1521), when prosperity was high due to the Voyages of Discovery and the beginning of the market in gold, ivory, precious stones and spice from the East. Although the design of much of Portugal's architecture had been inspired by France and Spain, the Manueline style – which was closely allied to the Late Gothic – was drawn from the influences of both Portuguese India and Moorish architecture. It was the first instance in Western history of a non-European influence on European architecture.

The dominant features of the Manueline style are ropes, shells, anchors, seaweed, exotic and indigenous plants, and the concentric circles reminiscent of the first marine charts used by the navigators to make their astronomical calculations. The Cross of the Order of Christ (Maltese Cross) also forms part of the decorative theme, and in many instances the Manueline shield is featured.

CLIMATE

The Atlantic influence on the Mediterranean-type climate of southern Portugal tempers the heat in summer and warms the shores in winter.

Winters are mild on the coastline, with occasional frost on low-lying ground. During summer the heat is moderated by onshore winds. Inland, winters can be more severe, with snow appearing very occasionally on the summit of Monchique.

Summer can be especially hot in the Alentejo plains, where temperatures reach 40°C, but humidity at least remains low. Hours of sunshine average 3,500 annually on the coastline, but are somewhat fewer in the mountainous areas.

Annual rainfall in the south is 466mm, but in the Caldeirão and Monchique mountains is considerably higher, with some years accumulating more than 1,000mm. Rainfall in the grain-growing Alentejo plains is much lower.

The rains usually begin at the end of September, leading up to the heavy autumnal downfalls at the end of October and November. Over the Christmas period and early part of the year the weather is frequently mild and much drier. The spring rainfall lasts from the end of January to the end of April, but rarely are there days with a continuous downpour. The summer period is virtually completely free of rain.

HABITAT TYPES

Mountain

The 902m Serra de Monchique has a distinctive habitat. The lower reaches are very fertile, with deep black soil fed by many streams. Higher up, scrub and plantations of Maritime Pine, eucalyptus and Cork Oak take over, and above 600m the land becomes treeless and covered with cistus scrub: mainly Gum and Salvia-leaved Cistus, *Cistus crispus* and on the woodland edges the acid-loving Poplar-leaved Cistus.

Evergreen Forest and Cistus Scrub

This covers vast tracts, especially in the Caldeirão region. The evergreen oak is predominately the Cork Oak while the cistus scrub is mainly Gum Cistus, but in some regions there are large quantities of Narrow-leaved or Grey-leaved Cistus.

Azure-winged Magpies and the Magpie, showing the difference in size. The Azure-winged Magpie has a strange geographical distribution. It is only found in south-west Iberia, China and Japan, and was possibly introduced to Iberia during the 16th century by Portuguese sailors returning from voyages to the Far East.

TYPICAL ANIMALS AND PLANTS OF THE MAIN HABITATS

MOUNTAIN

PLANT LIFE
Many interesting plants flourish in more exposed areas:
• *Paeonia broteroi*
• *Rhododendron ponticum* subsp. *baeticum*
• *Drosophyllum lusitanicum* in the woodlands
• Orchids, including the minute Dense-flowered Orchid which, surprisingly, is found here between the rocks, rather than growing on limestone as it does in Ireland.
• Heathers
• Foxglove
• *Dianthus*
• *Tuberaria guttata*.

BIRDLIFE
During autumn:
• Short-toed Eagle
• Booted Eagle
• Griffon Vulture
Migratory:
• Rock Thrush
• Whinchat
Resident:
• Golden and Bonelli's Eagles
• Blue Rock Thrush
• Rock Bunting
• Dartford and Sardinian Warblers
• Long-tailed, Crested and Great Tits
• Azure-winged Magpie
• Stonechat
• Woodpeckers and Jays all inhabit the woodland.

BUTTERFLIES
Butterflies are common, especially the following:
• Swallowtail
• Clouded Yellow
• Spanish Marbled White
• Cleopatra
• Spanish Festoon (early in the season)
• Two-tailed Pasha.

EVERGREEN FOREST AND CISTUS SCRUB

BIRDLIFE
• Woodpeckers: Great Spotted and Green are the most common, but also the sparrow-sized Lesser Spotted, which is local.
• Short-toed Treecreepers, Nuthatch and Azure-winged Magpies are found in the woodland.
• Golden Orioles (migratory) can be heard 'mewing', accompanied by Nightingale (migratory) and Blackcap (resident) songs.
• Bee-eaters (migratory) fly overhead, while Serins sing high in the trees with Melodious (migratory), Dartford and Sardinian Warblers lower down.
• Greenfinch and Cirl Bunting, Woodlarks and Great, Blue, Crested and Long-tailed Tits, Jays and the uncommon Rufous Bushchat (migratory) can all be seen.

BUTTERFLIES
• Swallowtail
• Two-tailed Pasha
• Scarce Swallowtail
• Great Banded Grayling
• Spanish Gatekeeper
• Speckled Wood
• Blue-spot and Green Hairstreak
• Small Copper
• Long-tailed Blue
• Lang's Short-tailed Blue.

MAMMALS
The following are present but not often seen:
• Wild Boar
• Egyptian Mongoose
• Genet
• Red Fox
• Rabbit.

STEPPE

BIRDLIFE
• Great and Little Bustards
• Black-bellied Sandgrouse (elusive)
• Stone Curlew
• Short-toed, Calandra and Crested Larks
• Montagu's Harrier (summer)
• Hen Harrier (winter; rare)
• Kestrel
• Lesser Kestrel (summer)
• Short-toed and Golden Eagles
• White Stork
• Great Grey Shrike (resident)
• Woodchat Shrike (migratory).

MAMMALS
Few mammals inhabit this area, although you may find:
• Wild Boar
• Egyptian Mongoose
• Rabbit.

RIVER

BIRDLIFE
• Common Sandpiper
• Little Ringed Plover (migratory)
• Fan-tailed Warbler
• Great Reed Warbler (migratory)
• Bee-eater (migratory)
• Kingfisher
• Blue-headed Yellow Wagtail (migratory)
• Chiffchaff (migratory)
• Garden Warbler
• Wren
• Little Egret.

MAMMALS
• Otters are relatively common.
• Egyptian Mongoose, Genet and Beech Marten are all present but rarely seen.

TYPICAL ANIMALS AND PLANTS OF THE MAIN HABITATS continued

SEA CLIFF

PLANT LIFE

Many endemic plants can be found in the sand dunes:
- *Thymus camphoratus*
- *Cistus palhinhae* (sticky leaved)
- *Antirrhinum majus* var. *linkianum*
- *Viola arborescens* (winter flowering)
- *Linaria algarviana*
- *Corema alba*

Also found are:
- Blue Shrubby Pimpernel
- Spiny *Astragalus massiliensis*
- Several *Orobanche* species, usually parasitizing leguminous plants
- Low-growing juniper bushes
- Many bulbous and rhizomatous plants
- Orchids
- Tulips
- Narcissi
- Irises
- Asphodels
- Sea Daffodil.

BIRDLIFE

The following all nest in crevices in the cliffs:
- Blue Rock Thrush
- Black Redstart
- Alpine Swift (migratory)
- Shag
- Rock Dove
- Chough
- Jackdaw

During migration:
- Gannet
- Cory's Shearwater
- Razorbill.

Osprey often winter here and, strangely, the Alpine Accentor often winters on Cabo de São Vicente.

INSECTS

Worth a mention are the unusual Ribbon-tailed Lacewing and the Six-spot Burnet, both of which are commonly seen, as are many butterflies.

SALT MARSH

PLANT LIFE

Unusual halophytic plants grow in the marshes, including the beautiful *Cistanche phelypaea* with its large spectacular yellow-flowered spikes and the strange but rare *Cynomorium coccineum*, both of which are parasitic on species of *Chenopodium*. Sea Lavender and Sea Stock are prolific.

BIRDLIFE

Many migrating birds feed in these marshes, with a large number remaining to breed, thus swelling the resident population to many thousands.

Black-winged Stilts, Avocets, Little Terns and Kentish Plover all breed on the sandy beaches and salt-pan retaining banks.

The Gum Cistus, used by IN LOCO as their logo, covers thousands of hectares of hillside and scrublands. The plants are periodically cut, dried and burnt as fuel for village bread ovens. They are also used to produce a greenish-brown dye for cotton and linen goods.

Freshly cut cork, once it has been graded, is stacked to cure in the open air for a year before going to the factory for processing. Here it is heaped on a disused football ground – the 'drift to the towns' has left the village inhabited by only the older generation.

Steppe

This is a typical habitat of the northern Algarve and Baixo Alentejo. It basically consists of degenerate vegetation where low rainfall combined with overgrazing by sheep and goats has led to erosion. In many places the land is farmed with cereals, which has somewhat alleviated the situation by giving some ground cover. With the winter rains comes a mass of annuals, which rapidly grow and flower, giving an ever-changing vista.

Sea Cliff

These high cliffs on the west coast are treeless, but covered with sand dunes, which provide a special habitat.

The rolling grasslands in the southern part of the Mértola concelho are green in spring but parched ochre in the summer. Countless numbers of the Campaniça (Merino type) sheep are grazed here and are milked daily for cheese production during winter and spring.

The wild and dangerous coastline of Cabo Sardão, where the hard Carboniferous slate interspersed with veins of quartz reaches the sea. This is an interesting area not only for plants, but for sea birds which can often be seen offshore during the migration period.

River

Many waterways are thick with the Giant Reed, which gives a very special environment for Marsh Frogs, European Pond Terrapins, Spiny-ribbed Salamanders, Viperine and Grass Snakes and many dragonflies and damselflies.

The Ribeira do Vascão divides the Algarve from the Alentejo and makes a delightful place for a picnic. A walk along the north-eastern bank passes two river mills, the first deserted and the second, Azenha do Alferes in the São Sebastião dos Carros *freguesia*, recently restored.

Most small rivers in southern Portugal dry up during the summer months, leaving just a fine silty bed with a few perennial pools much frequented by passing birds and flocks of goats or sheep. In late summer the beautiful indigenous, single pink Oleander grows in profusion.

Salt Marsh

Marshes stretch along the southern Algarve coast, with several inlets on the western end and a huge expanse along the eastern end producing a very delicate habitat.

The Wild Boar, possibly the region's most common large mammal, is certainly the most widespread. Nocturnal, it spends its days hidden in woodland or scrub, but emerges at night to ravage gardens and golf courses! Very occasionally it ventures onto deserted beaches to forage on the high tide line.

DOMESTIC LIVESTOCK IN SOUTHERN PORTUGAL

Southern Portugal has few large commercial livestock units, although recently besides traditional farming, the rearing of Ostriches for meat and leather, as well as Red Deer, Red-legged Partridge and Pheasant for sporting purposes has begun.

The small farming communities still rely largely on their own produce, and farmsteads keep working animals plus innumerable varieties of poultry.

Cattle

The indigenous bovine of this area is the Alentejano Chamusco, a large, heavily built, deep red animal with moderately wide horns. It is traditionally a multipurpose animal bred for meat, milk and farm work such as pulling carts, ploughing and general cultivation.

In the Baixo Alentejo are the Mertolenga Malhado, with its white rear quarters and heavily blotched fore-end, and the Mertolenga Rosilho-mil-flores, which is similar but with very fine spotted frontal marks. These animals are generally of finer build and are used mainly for beef production in much larger units.

Recently Charolais and Limousin from France have been successfully introduced to improve quality. Occasionally Holstein cattle are seen that are either pure or crossbred, and in the Odemira *concelho* some large irrigated units produce milk for the local dairy.

Donkeys, Mules and Horses

The traditional form of transport, especially in rural areas, is by donkey, carrying their owners or transporting straw, corn, cork, water or other lightweight produce, leaving heavier work to mules. In southern Portugal the donkeys are usually rather small, but further north on vast estates they are larger, with strains of Spanish blood. Usually grey or dark brown in colour, they often have a dark stripe along the back and across the shoulders. Panniers or frames are fitted over coarse saddles according to the goods being carried, and can be highly decorated with coloured wool and small bells.

Mules here are usually the offspring of a jack donkey and a mare, rarely a stallion and a she-ass (which produces a hinny). As mules and hinnies are bigeneric hybrids, they are sterile. Hardy and very strong, they are used for ploughing, pulling carts and all heavy work unsuitable for donkeys.

Horses are used for herding cattle and sheep in more extensive pastoral areas of the Alentejo, but are used sparingly in hilly regions. In tourist areas they are more common as mounts in riding schools. The Lusitano and Alter Real are well-known Portuguese breeds.

Sheep

There are basically two breeds of sheep in southern Portugal: the coarse-coated Algarvio Churro and the much heavier Campaniça (Merino type), which is found more frequently in the Baixo Alentejo.

The attractive, long-horned Churro with black markings on the face and limbs is long legged and has coarse white wool of poor quality which is used mainly for the manufacture of rugs, carpets and blankets. Its main attribute is that it is very prolific and produces two or three lambs annually, which reach a weight of 25–30kg in 3–4 months, when most are sold for meat. Some are kept until they are 8–10 months old, when they weigh 45–50kg.

Historically, this breed originated from the Lebrijano or Marismeno in adjacent

The attractive Churro sheep is the typical long-legged, coarse-coated breed seen in flocks throughout the southern part of the Algarve. With their propensity to thrive and fatten on poor pasture and scrubland they are very popular.

Spain. Today there are about 30,000 pure breeds in the Algarve, which forage and live on poor hillside scrub where other breeds fail to flourish.

The Alentejo's large flocks of Campaniça are known for fine, high-quality wool and prolific milk production. After the lambs have been weaned the ewes are milked by hand, twice daily. All the milk is made into cheese, which is famous throughout Portugal.

Goats
The single-coloured Charnequeira and the bearded Serpentina are Alentejo breeds, the latter a pale colour with a heavy dark dorsal stripe, dark head and dark under-parts.

The Algarve breed has developed over the years from the Charnequeira and imported stock from Spain and Morocco. It is a very old, hardy breed which feeds on the cistus scrubland to produce a strong

23

animal weighing 40–50kg for females and 60–80kg for males. In colour the animals are white, mottled with well-defined areas of black or brown and often spotted.

This is a prolific breed, and one male running with 45 females can sire over 70 per cent of twin births. Kids produced in winter benefit from grass and plants which grow well after the autumn rains. The birth weight is usually 2.3–2.5kg. For meat they are sold at 8–10kg, which they reach in 45 to 60 days. Their milk is used for delicious local cheese, which is a major source of income. Milked by hand twice daily, they have been known to produce 730 litres of milk in a 204-day lactation.

In January 1991 the *Associação Nacional dos Criadores de Caprinos da Raça Algarvia* (ANCCRAL), the breed society of the Algarve goat, was initiated, and in 1992 a herd book was formed with about 22,000 entries. ANCCRAL also helps with the much needed marketing of meat and cheese.

Pigs
White pigs, mainly Large White and Landrace, are used in commercial pig farms, mostly in the valleys of the Serra de Monchique.

In the Alentejo oak woods, herds of black cross-breeds or Alentejano black pigs can still be seen foraging for acorns (which help to give a delicious flavour to hams and *chouriças*), attended by a swineherd. These pigs are usually shorter and very much fatter than their north European white counterpart.

Portuguese or Algarve Water Dog
The Portuguese or Algarve Water Dog (as it is often called) is a lovely creature, usually black, but occasionally brown or white, or combinations of black and white or brown and white. Similar to a Standard Poodle in form, its muzzle, loin and hind quarters are clipped, with the hair at the end of the tail left untrimmed. One specific characteristic is a membrane between the toes (they are said to have 'webbed feet'), which helps to make the dogs unparalleled swimmers and divers of enormous stamina. They are also excellent guard dogs and companions, especially to the fishermen to whom they are an invaluable helpmate, notably retrieving fish if they escape from the nets or hooks by diving to depths of up to 6m. Equally, they will swim to shore with ropes for tying up boats, or retrieve broken nets or lines out at sea.

Some years ago, these practically extinct pedigree dogs were almost all sold to the United States. Today, though, the *Serviço Nacional de Parques, Reservas e Conservação da Natureza* at the integral Quinta de Marim in the Ria Formosa Reserve is breeding this splendid race to improve the species and regain its high quality.

The sheepdogs in the area are a strange crossbred group, some of the larger ones showing their ancestry to the Rafeiro do Alentejo, and smaller 'woolly' ones to the Cão da Serra de Aires. Many of the hunting dogs have the unmistakable stamp of the elegant Portuguese Pointer (*Perdigueiro Português*).

Rabbits
Although a number of commercial rabbit enterprises have been established recently using imported white furred varieties, home production of rabbits still remains part of the country tradition, even with the advent of myxomatosis, for which treatment is now given. Hutches or small barns are used for housing and producing sufficient young for a family's needs. The rabbits are of mixed races and are fed almost entirely on food from the surrounding countryside.

Poultry
Renowned breeds of white-feathered chickens, turkeys and ducks are now bred

and reared for meat in some commercial enterprises in southern Portugal, with corresponding lighter weight breeds of hens used for egg production. They are all basically fed on rations with a high maize content, giving rise not only to meat which is much more yellow than is generally accepted in some countries, but also to egg yolks of a deep golden colour.

In rural areas you can still see what is generally regarded as a country farmyard, with arrogant cockerels guarding their hens, many of the latter looking as if they have had their necks plucked. These birds are indigenous to the area and are reputed to be better egg layers.

Colourful, proud bantam cocks with their unobtrusive unicolour mates are also bred. The latter will sit tightly to incubate a maximum of six hen's eggs and then become conscientious mothers.

Black, fan-tailed turkeys are also here, but since the arrival of their more sophisticated 'farmed', white-plumaged counterpart, it is now rare to see them herded in their hundreds over the Alentejo plains.

Heavy, dark-fleshed Muscovy Ducks also have their place, and a Mallard crossbred is in evidence in some locations.

A breeding trio of the natural sex-linked geese, not far removed from their Greylag ancestors, is part of the rural tradition, and many farmsteads still have the flighty, noisy Guinea Fowl. Roosting in trees, it incessantly gives its 'pa-ta-ca, pa-ta-ca' call, hence the local name of 'Pataca'.

Pigeons

Pigeons are considered a great delicacy and can still be found in many farmyards and often on the menu in rural restaurants. Throughout the region, you will also see large flocks of racing pigeons recently released from their lofts. They compete in frequent races from Lisbon, Madrid and Oporto.

MEASURES TO ASSIST THE PEOPLE

The entire area of the Caldeirão was ignored by the rest of Portugal for a long time, receiving no benefit from the growth process which was experienced in Lisbon and Oporto and along the Algarve coastline from the 1960s onwards. This situation aggravated the gap between city and country areas, and caused an acute exodus of people from the villages, especially the younger generation, for whom lack of employment prospects and precarious living conditions led to a feeling of isolation. Not surprisingly, they were drawn to the cities.

Twenty years ago, living conditions were difficult, with electricity, running water and sewage systems exceptional luxuries. Since the authoritarian political regime of Salazar and Caetano was toppled in 1974, improvements have been – and continue to be – made, although at a slower pace than in the tourist resorts. With the establishment of democratically elected local authorities, more attention is being paid to the standard of local life. Electricity and telephones have become widespread, and health centres are now a normal feature of most Parish Councils.

After Portugal's entry into the European Union (formerly European Community), the road network was dramatically improved throughout the whole country, with the benefit being felt even in the remote areas of the Caldeirão. Despite these improvements, however, cement and asphalt alone could not keep people in the villages, and the general feeling in the mid-1980s was that more had to be done, particularly with regard to local income-generating initiatives and cultural, social and environmental activities.

In October 1985, a group of local people from Faro formed the RADIAL Project with the help of the Dutch Foundation Bernard van Leer and later that of several local authorities, regional branches of the Education, Employment and Social Affairs Departments, and the University of the Algarve. This made possible small but significant local initiatives, including children's centres and women's workshops in Alte, Cachopo, Azinhal and Martinlongo. The project had an immediate real impact, which not only improved the living standards of many women and children, but also revealed to the local people that it was, indeed, possible to improve their situation.

Following the European Commission's creation of LEADER, an important initiative for rural development throughout Europe, in March 1991, the Association IN LOCO, which was created in 1988 to formalize the RADIAL Project, was able to submit to Brussels a Local Development Plan, which was approved eight months later. The result has been that since early 1992, this association, in partnership with municipalities, public bodies and private enterprises and associations, has co-financed over a hundred local projects aimed at revitalizing the Serra do Caldeirão.

Help has also been approved for rural tourism, and studies on marketing, *medronho* and cheese making, fruit drying and honey production, to mention just a few, have been carried out to assist local artisans and produce suppliers. The development of an outlet for these products is also high up on the list. Several artisan and produce exhibitions are held annually, both in the Algarve and at other events throughout the country. The opening of *Casa da Serra* shops in Salir (1993) and Faro (1994), where only products from this depressed region are sold, has given further encouragement to local initiatives.

In addition to the above assistance, many of the local *concelhos* give help in various forms, including setting up training and loaning workshops in venues such as disused primary schools. The IEFP (*Instituto de Emprego e Formação Profissional*) also offers intensive training schemes.

Although the northern Algarve and southern Alentejo are famous for weaving, many locals find marketing their craft one of their biggest problems. In many instances they are assisted through craft exhibitions and other outlets, and some people have had their ancient family looms replaced with help from IN LOCO or local councils.

CONSERVATION OF WILDLIFE

Throughout Portugal there are numerous protected areas, including National Parks, Natural Parks, Natural Reserves, protected countryside and classified sites, all of which are controlled by the SNPRCN (*Serviço Nacional de Parques, Reservas e Conservação da Natureza*). Besides this organization, there are several national and local groups all working to protect Portugal's natural heritage.

Within this region of southern Portugal there are three important zones with many classified sites. The largest is along the west coast, from Sines southwards to Sagres and then eastwards to Burgau. This 70,000ha area was designated to protect the unique flora, which includes a large number of endemic plants and also extends to a 2km maritime area known as *Área de Paisagem Protegida do Sudoeste Alentejano e Costa Vicentina*. Its administrative offices are in Odemira and Aljezur.

The 18,400ha *Parque Natural da Ria Formosa* protects the delicate flora and fauna of the salt marshes which stretch for 60km from Ancão near Quinta do Lago to Cacela a Velha. Within this park is the integral Quinta de Marim with its large information, research and bird rehabilitation centres, which make this the foremost such centre in southern Portugal.

The *Reserva Natural do Sapal de Castro Marim e Vila Real de Santo António* in the eastern Algarve has an information centre in the castle at Castro Marim. Again, it preserves marshes and working salt evaporating pans, which are home to a large number of wetland birds, including the beautiful Greater Flamingo, Spoonbills and Avocets. The woods near Monte Gordo are a stronghold of the heavily protected Chameleon.

The Sawfly Orchid is one of the earliest – and one of the most beautiful – orchids to flower, usually in late February. All species of orchid are protected to preserve their beauty for future generations and should never be picked or dug up.

Classified sites include the Fonte da Benémola and Rocha da Pena, with more locations being added annually.

Hunting (shooting) is restricted to Thursdays, Sundays and public holidays during the open season. The main quarry is Turtle Dove during the annual autumn migration, but many species are fully protected. Red-legged Partridge, Rabbit, duck and the protected Wild Boar is culled under licence when numbers become excessive. Hunting is controlled throughout the country: red and white metal markers by the roadside indicate that hunting is forbidden in the area beyond.

Recently, large properties have been turned into enclosed shooting reserves for either tourists or associations. Throughout the southern Alentejo and parts of the Algarve where large properties predominate, almost 242,000ha have been reserved for this purpose (either *turística* or *associativa*), thus easing the task of wildlife management. Such reserves are not without their drawbacks, however, for they can be detrimental to rural development and hamper traditional grazing. Another problem is the threat to birds of prey (which are themselves protected) and predatory mammals, which are perceived as being a threat to the reserves.

Small bird trapping is outlawed and wardens diligently patrol many areas; traps are confiscated and offenders punished.

GENERAL TIPS

Climate
The best time to travel to the interior regions is any time apart from summer, which can be extremely hot. In winter the weather is occasionally wet, but this is nonetheless a lovely time to travel: the rain does not usually last for long and there are invariably extensive periods of warm sun.

Spring is particularly beautiful, with the fields coloured by annual flowers, and is certainly the best time to visit the coastal and other limestone regions for the great variety of flora.

The light for photography is extremely clear and bright, so do take this into account to obtain the best from your holiday pictures.

Clothing
Do remember that the evenings can be cool, so bring a sweater. The lower temperatures are in fact more conducive to a good night's sleep.

Bird Watching
Birding is possible throughout the year, with migratory birds in spring and autumn in particular, wintering birds in the estuaries and many beautiful summer visitors throughout the region. Winter is a good time to see Little and Great Bustards in the interior before the cereals have grown too high to hide them from view.

Crafts
If you want to visit artisans, any weekday is suitable and they are always delighted to see you.

Walking
The general rule for walking through the countryside is that you can go anywhere, as long as there are no fences or barriers encircling the land. Under no circumstances should you attempt to cross land with crops or other cultivated areas.

Food and Drink
Food on tourist routes is available everywhere (it is always an idea to look for a large number of Portuguese-owned cars outside eating establishments, which indicates excellent food at very reasonable prices). In the interior, good food is available on the through routes, and sandwiches can usually be supplied with cool drinks in the more remote areas. For a lunch-time snack ask for a *bifana*, a tasty slice of thin, hot pork in either delicious local bread or a *paposeco* (bread roll).

Throughout, drinks are available in local tavernas and are always served chilled.

For coffee lovers a *bica* is a small, very strong, black coffee.

Water

Water is generally drinkable, but you may prefer to buy delicious spring water in the non-returnable five-litre plastic containers.

Accommodation and Information

Large towns along the coastal strip have tourist centres where information on hotels, campsites and other accommodation can be obtained. In smaller towns which have no tourist information, local restaurants are often extremely helpful.

Medical Care

It is always sensible to carry a first-aid kit for emergencies. Chemists (*farmácias*) in Portugal can supply many more medicines without prescription than in Britain, but the hassle of trying to buy them in a foreign language is difficult, especially if you consider that to be *constipado* is to have a head cold!

Bring all necessary sun creams. The air is unpolluted and sunburn can be painful and dangerous.

Mosquitoes are present in some areas. They are not malarial, but bites can cause considerable irritation and an insect repellent is advisable.

There is little need to worry about bites from snakes, scorpions or other venomous creatures, but in the unlikely event of this happening go to the local hospital, clinic or doctor as quickly as possible.

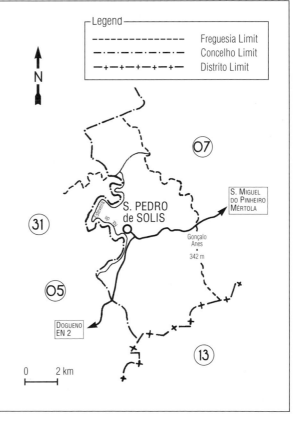

KEY TO THE MAPS

Each of the 27 *freguesias* and 18 *concelhos* in the following two sections has an accompanying map like this one. North points up the page and the scale is as here unless otherwise shown by the map. The different types of regional boundaries are as shown in the legend.

Bgem	dam or reservoir
R. or Rio	river
Ra	small river or stream
Mirador	belvedere
Anta	dolmen
Azenha	water-mill
Rocha	rock
Algar	cave
Fonte or Fte	fountain
Cerro	hill

Legend
------------------- Freguesia Limit
—·—·—·—·—·— Concelho Limit
—+—+—+—+—+— Distrito Limit

N

S. PEDRO de SOLIS

S. MIGUEL DO PINHEIRO MÉRTOLA

Gonçalo Anes
342 m

DOGUENO EN 2

0   2 km

SECTION 2
CALDEIRÃO
MOUNTAIN
REGION

The 27 sites in this section cover all of the *freguesias* (parish councils) that are being helped by IN LOCO with the assistance of the European Union. They are of varying sizes, ranging from villages with a few outlying hamlets, like Pereiro (no. 15), Giões (14) and Gomes Aires (02), to small towns such as Almodôvar (04), São Bartolomeu de Messines (17) and São Brás de Alportel (26).

This is an incredibly beautiful area, completely unspoilt by the modern intrusions you might expect so close to the Algarve coastline. Historically, it has a lot to offer. The people themselves are delightful, and the help they are being given is bringing back a stability to the region which had previously been eroded. Visitors to the area will undoubtedly help even more.

All of these communities are situated within the Caldeirão mountain range, which straddles the north-eastern Algarve and south-eastern Alentejo. Most of them do not lie on the usual tourist routes and are experiencing an exodus of the younger generation, men in particular, who are leaving to seek a better income from either the tourist coastline or from foreign sources such as France, Germany and the USA. In the Alentejo section, the main

In more remote areas of the Serra do Caldeirão these round conical homes were still used as dwelling houses 150 years ago. Now they are used as stores. The style is Celtic and they are identical to the Celtic homes in the Shetlands, the Western Isles, Ireland and Galicia.

A donkey with its light-weight load of dried cistus scrub for fuelling the bread ovens.

income is generated from cork, which is cut every nine years, or from *rosmaninho* honey from Green and French Lavender, which is collected annually. This, by anyone's standards, is a poor existence.

The crops in the south are sparse, and are invariably restricted to steep hillsides, which demand harvesting by hand with a sickle. Goats and – on more level ground with better grazing – sheep are kept, the flocks being herded in the same way as in biblical times. The shepherd, with his assorted group of obedient and loyal dogs, spends his waking hours following the grazing animals from hill to hill and pasture to pasture. His is a hard and lonely life, relieved only by the changing seasons and the inevitable cycle of life and death within the flock.

The population is mainly of the older generation, many of whom neither read nor write. Although the younger men are moving away, wives are often left behind to look after the children. Thanks to assistance, the women have been able to achieve much: the revival of dying crafts, the establishment of crèches for children, and above all the marketing of their produce, giving monetary reward for work well done and helping them to maintain their self respect through financial independence.

01 SANTANA DA SERRA

Santana da Serra is bounded by Odemira (28) to the west, Ourique (29) to the north, Gomes Aires (02) eastwards, and São Marcos da Serra (10) to the south. It is easily accessible from the Albufeira to Lisbon IP1 motorway.

Archaeology and Architecture

The area is archaeologically extremely interesting, with the Castro da Cola circuit about 10km north of the town (clearly marked from the IP1). An excellent map on a slope near Nossa Senhora da Cola church marks all of the sites, which cover 5,000 years of history and include the Arabic Castro da Cola. This fortified castle was active from the 8th to the 13th centuries, before finally being abandoned in the 14th century. Occupying an elevated vantage point near the church, much of the original construction is clearly visible.

The water mill on the Rio Mira is easily reached and lies in picturesque surroundings which are worth a visit in themselves. Also accessible are Copper and Bronze Age burial sites, which testify to occupation of the area between 3000BC and 1000BC. Throughout this region, excavations which began in the 18th century have continued spasmodically up until the present time.

If you want to visit the church in Santana da Serra, ask at the nearby house. Donations can be left in the offertory box in the church, and you may want to give a gratuity to the lady who shows you round.

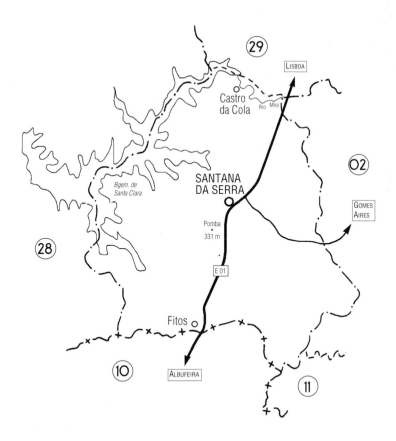

Landscape and Crops

The working windmill of Pomba was built in 1852 and, lying at 331m, enjoys a prominent position overlooking Santana da Serra, with Castro Verde and Ourique in the far distance. The mill reflects the agricultural prosperity of this area in past times, when wheat was grown extensively. Today, much of the land has been allowed to revert to scrubland and pasture, as it is too poor to yield an economic return from cereals.

The thin soil overlies a Carboniferous shale and slate bedrock. In the river and stream valleys, orchards and vegetables are grown, as are a few vines where there is sufficient depth of good loam.

Fauna, Flora and Birdlife

The slightly acidic soil produces a colourful array of flora during spring, when poppies, gladioli and Barbary Nut colour the countryside. The Green-winged Orchid is common throughout, its purple flowers contrasting strongly with the vivid blue Alkanet.

During spring, a wealth of butterflies can be seen, and their larvae feed within the pasture lands near the river. Common types include Red Admiral, Small and Marbled Whites, Speckled Wood and a variety of Blues. Scarce Swallowtail and the Swallowtail are found especially where Fennel grows.

A number of animals find shelter on the hillsides in the predominantly Gum Cistus covering. These include Rabbits, Red Foxes, Egyptian Mongoose and the Wild Boar, which hides in the valleys during the day and only emerges at night to forage for food.

Millstones beside the working windmill of Pomba, overlooking Santana da Serra. From here you can enjoy a fantastic panorama, including the main IP1 from Lisbon to the Algarve, which can be seen winding through the wooded hillsides with the vast Alentejo plains in the background.

The Barbary Nut, found throughout the southern region, is a familiar sight in springtime and often colours the road verges. The flower colour is very variable, from almost white through to deep purple. This is an unusual plant, as the flowers only open during the afternoon.

34

Here also Cork and Ilex Oaks (variety *rotundifolia*) grow, the roots working their way into rock fissures to find nourishment. The cork is harvested commercially, while the Ilex Oak provides wood for furniture and high-quality charcoal. Large flocks of sheep and goats graze the scrub and pasture, and herds of black pigs forage for acorns amongst the trees.

Crafts and Local Produce

If you've an eye for crafts, you'll enjoy seeing the incredible wood carvings made by Rui Miguel Guerreiro from Fitos village just south of Santana da Serra. He mainly uses Brazilian woods, because he finds the local oak much too hard to work.

Alternatively, head for Santana da Serra, where the *artesanato* signs lead to the ceramic workshop of Carlos Mateus. Carlos is a talented artist who depicts

countryside traditions on plates and tiles in his distinctive style. Pastoral scenes of shepherds minding their sheep, specialists cutting cork bark, bread making or the traditional collection of honey from old-fashioned cork beehives are just some of the traditional ways of life that are commemorated in his work. These and others, like cutting cereals by sickle, are lifestyles which are fast disappearing.

Carlos's wife, Alexandra, paints in a more formal style, mainly in the traditional colours of blue and white. Their plates, bowls and tiles are first covered with a white liquid (slip), before the design is pencilled in. This is then painted, prior to rinsing in a solution of powdered glass for glazing, and then fired in the oven for nine or ten hours at 990°C. (The temperature must not be raised more than 100°C per hour for the first 300°C, and equally, when decreasing, the oven doors must not be opened before the temperature has slowly dropped to below 300°C, otherwise the rush of cold air will cause breakages.)

Carlos also makes cork spoons and small barrel-shaped containers which were traditionally used for carrying food in the fields (keeping it warm in winter and cool in summer). In addition, he produces attractive small, painted cork cottages.

Honey and *medronho* production are important within this area, and Carlos's neighbour has 700 beehives. The bees feed on the colourful French and Green Lavenders, the highly flavoured nectar of which helps to produce a delicious final result. As in many regions, Santana da Serra's bakery produces fine home-made bread.

In the town itself is the attractive typical blue and white cottage of potters Carlos and his wife Alexandra. They have many interesting designs, their latest pieces being made of local slate, painted with chimneys or cottages and using the form of the slate to enhance the finished article.

02 GOMES AIRES

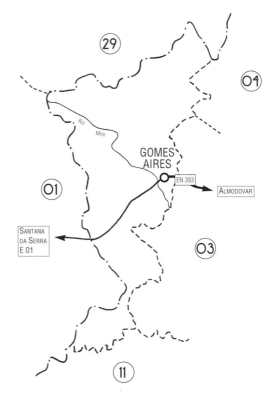

Gomes Aires is bounded to the north by Ourique (29), to the east by Almodôvar (04) and Santa-Clara-a-Nova (03), to the south by São Barnabé (11), and to the west by Santana da Serra (01). It is accessible from Almodôvar on the EN393, which intersects the Albufeira to Lisbon motorway just north of Santana da Serra.

Archaeology and Architecture
This is a village of white houses, many of which are of the typical low, adobe design with Roman-style pantile roofs. The impressive parish church lies in the centre of the winding streets and is approached by a series of steep steps.

Landscape and Crops
The surrounding countryside is wild and remote. It occupies the western side of the Caldeirão mountain watershed and is transversed by the young Rio Mira. Thin soil overlies hard slate and schist which supports little cultivation, but extensive

grassland dotted with the *rotundifolia* variety of the Ilex Oak gives a parkland scene. This sub-species of oak produces a sweet acorn (known as *bolota*), in contrast to the usual bitter flavoured one with its high tannin content (found in Central and Eastern Spain). The *bolota* is a substantial source of food for herds of the black Alentejano pigs which are reared in this area for meat, especially hams and *chouriça*. These nuts are also eaten roasted by the local population.

The trees are pruned periodically into an impressive flat-topped open form, and the wood is used for making very high-quality charcoal.

Fauna, Flora and Birdlife

Buzzards are frequently spotted high on the thermals looking for small mammals and birds. The thick canopy of the oak trees provides cover for Azure-winged Magpies, Great Spotted Woodpeckers and the summer-visiting Golden Orioles. In the scrub many warblers feed, including Sardinian, Dartford and the yellowish Melodious with its heavier looking crown, typical of the *Hippolais* group. In Iberia, the Melodious Warbler replaces the Icterine Warbler of Eastern Europe. Both the resident Great Grey and the migratory Woodchat Shrikes pounce on grasshoppers, while Bee-eaters are common near streams, where they often nest in the sandy banks like Kingfishers. The Hoopoe flaps lazily between the trees, its flamboyant crest stiffening as it lands to probe for insects in the moist soil. Its onomatopoeic call means that it is often heard long before it is seen, camouflaged surprisingly well within the decaying leaves.

Crafts and Local Produce

Local crafts include baskets made from bamboo cut in the river valleys and beautiful crochet work.

Cattle, sheep and goats feed in the grasslands, producing milk for cheese. Honey is an important commodity, and many hundreds of hives are taken into the hillsides, where the bees gather nectar from Green and French Lavender. Fertilizers and chemicals are rarely used, and the pure, unadulterated honey is highly prized. Traditional hives made from cork bark can still be found in places.

Left Typical charcoal burning. These smoking heaps can be seen throughout the southern Alentejo wooded regions and on the northern slopes of Monchique. The main wood is from the Ilex Oak. The trees are pruned periodically and produce the finest charcoal.

Right A young goatherd proudly showing his favourite 'nanny'. Goats are milked twice daily and their milk used for delicious cheese. Two kinds of pedigree goats are bred in the Alentejo: the single-coloured Charnequeira and the bearded Serpentina, which has a dark spinal stripe on a pale base.

Cork beehives are still seen on some of the more remote hillsides, usually in long lines. These are made from a complete circle of stripped cork which is capped with another piece. Unlike the modern ones which are now more popular, they have no internal frames for the honey, only a cross beam.

Chouriça production throughout the region covered by this book is traditionally an autumn occupation. The pork meat, a mixture of lean and fat, is coarsely chopped and mixed with paste made from either large red, sweet peppers or, occasionally, red pepper and garlic. Natural skins are filled with this mixture, and the sausages are then tied with string and hung over smoking oak wood for two to three weeks until they are cured. (Commercially produced *chouriça* near to Salir (20) is prepared in the same way, but the sausages are boiled for ten minutes before being smoked for four days.)

Presunto hams are another local speciality. These are weighed and then salted for approximately fifteen days (a rule of thumb states that it should be one day per kilogram).

Many cottages in the area still have their huge, wide chimneys for *chouriça* smoking. Often the meat is marinated for a number of days in a mixture of vinegar and white wine with chopped garlic, salt, sweet red pepper paste and bay leaf, before the skins are filled and smoked as above.

If you look in local ceramic shops anywhere in the region, but particularly in Santana da Serra (01), you'll probably notice small oval dishes with bars across the top. These are for cooking *chouriça*. The sausage is placed on the bars and flamed with *medronho*, thus giving a delicious flavour.

03 SANTA-CLARA-A-NOVA

This is a triangular shaped *freguesia*, with Gomes Aires (02) to the west, Almodôvar (04) eastwards and São Barnabé (11) to the south. It is characterized by many small, modern, white houses and has a pretty little church. It is accessible from the Almodôvar to Gomes Aires EN393 road, with hard-core tracks winding into the countryside.

Archaeology and Architecture
Although the *freguesia* is tiny, it is extremely important, partly because it has been chosen as the site of a new archeological museum which, when it opens shortly, will house some of the most notable findings in Southern Portugal.

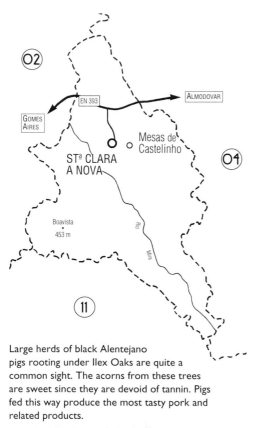

Large herds of black Alentejano
pigs rooting under Ilex Oaks are quite a
common sight. The acorns from these trees
are sweet since they are devoid of tannin. Pigs
fed this way produce the most tasty pork and
related products.

Nearby, Mesas de Castelinho (a small
Muslim castle) was excavated in the late
1980s and early 1990s, financed partly by
SOMINCOR (the company working the
Neves Corvo copper mine) and IPPAR (The
Portuguese Heritage Institute of Architec-
ture and Archaeology).

The project has unearthed articles dating
from between 500BC and AD150, the eras of
pre-Roman and Roman occupation. These
include pieces of tableware from Italy and
fragments of wine amphorae from Southern
Spain and Italy, as well as a bronze coin
minted in Myrtilis (the Roman name for
Mértola; 32) and many remnants of glass
necklaces and cooking utensils.

These sensational findings, which are
still being studied, are from one of the first
sites of its kind in Southern Portugal, thus
making them important nationally as well
as regionally.

Landscape and Crops
This is an infrequently visited area on the
western slopes of the Serra do Caldeirão,
through which the young Rio Mira winds
its way to the reservoir at Santa-Clara-a-
Velha and the Atlantic Ocean at Vila Nova

de Milfontes. The small tributaries have cut deep valleys through the hard bedrock, and the relatively high rainfall gives sufficient moisture for Cork and Ilex Oak to flourish, but the poor soil and undulating terrain precludes intensive cereal production. The Strawberry Tree grows in profusion and to great proportions in the stream valleys, producing fruit for *medronho* distillation.

Fauna, Flora and Birdlife
The leaves of the Strawberry Tree are food for the larvae of the Two-tailed Pasha, one of the largest European butterflies, and just one of the many varieties which can be seen on the hillsides, including the Skipper group, Blues and Hairstreaks. The beautiful Green and the Blue-spot Hairstreaks fly early in the season and flit over the maquis scrub.

Sheep, goats and cattle graze between the Ilex and Cork Oaks, while flocks of Cattle Egrets feed on insects (mainly grasshoppers) around their feet. These birds, which are members of the Heron family, are relatively new to Portugal. They originally inhabited tropical areas of Africa and Asia, but during this century have grown in numbers and spread to the temperate climates in both Europe and the Americas.

Crafts and Local Produce
Cottage industries in the area include the distillation of *medronho*, the local firewater made from the fruit of the Strawberry Tree, honey production from the hives of bees kept in the surrounding countryside, and the production of both sheep's and goat's cheeses.

The Swallowtail is a common butterfly and has two to three broods annually, with the larvae feeding mainly on the commonly found Fennel. The Scarce Swallowtail with striped wings is also often seen.

Ethnological Museum

Perhaps more interesting – and certainly surprising to find – is a comparatively new ethnological museum, which is well worth a visit. Situated next door to the *Junta de Freguesia* (parish council offices) in the main street, it is open during office hours (with the key kept at the Junta).

Opened in 1988, the museum houses an impressive array of memorabilia of day-to-day life from times past. In the farming section there are various different types of yokes used with cattle, mules or donkeys, including an 1870 machine for 'beating' cereals on the threshing floors. Also, there is a donkey saddle from 1800 filled with rye straw, an 1820 leather saddle, a number of ploughs from 1850, 1910 and 1920, and some mule-drawn harrows.

More domestic items include a Roman-type balance, complete with weights known as *arráteis* (1 *arrátel* equalled 750g), and utensils used for producing wine, olive oil and bread. A huge *medronho* jar dated 1821 is similar to the oil jars which are seen around.

An illustrative 18th–19th-century 'alentejana' house shows the typical wide chimney which was used for smoking *chouriças*, *lingüiças* and *paios* (the various preserved pork sausages of the countryside). Small hand mills for grinding cereals, a cow's horn for carrying oil, olives and vinegar into the countryside, and bags for carrying bread are amongst the other items on display, in addition to ancient looms and other equipment for making linen and woollen goods.

Two of the more unusual exhibits are a Gum Cistus (*Estêva*) root with a 40cm circumference (the shrub was reputed to be 100

An authentic reproduction of an early 19th-century cottage room in the ethnological museum in Santa-Clara-a-Nova. A recent addition to this museum is a 1.5 sq metre model of a mule-powered water well, complete with the farmer working his land.

years old and 3m or more high) and a piece of cork estimated to be between eight and nine hundred years old.

04 ALMODÔVAR

Almodôvar is bounded by the remainder of Almodôvar *concelho* (31) to the north, Santa Cruz (05) eastwards, São Barnabé (11) to the south, and Gomes Aires (02) and Santa-Clara-a-Nova (03) to the west. Lying on the crossroads of the Faro to Lisbon EN2, the EN267 to Mértola, and the EN393 to Gomes Aires, it is easily accessible. This historically interesting *freguesia* and *concelho* capital has many archaeological sites which are as yet unexplored.

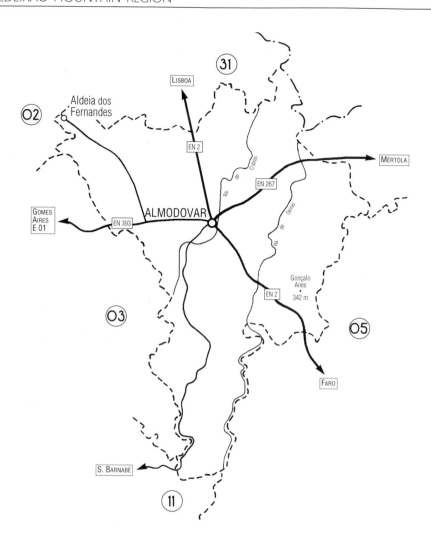

Archaeology and Architecture

The ancient palace, with 150cm thick walls, houses the town museum, which at one time was a prison, and the archives. The well preserved grill within the heavy wooden 'prison cell' cover shows how prisoners were incarcerated in the airless dungeons below. It is said that Dom Sebastião slept in the palace on his historic journey to Lagos in 1578, before leaving for North Africa and the disastrous battle of Alcacer Kabir.

The city charter was bestowed by Dom Dinis in 1285 and confirmed by Dom Manuel I on 1 June 1512.

A Roman bridge over the Ribeira de Cobres was renovated during the 1970s (it formed part of the important Via III during the 3rd century; *see p*age 13).

The 15th-century Misericórdia Church built under the orders of Dona Leonor, regent to Dom Afonso V, was restored in 1810 and again in 1980.

These are only a few of the interesting buildings within the town, which offers much to see. Even the thriving vegetable market, with its colourful *azulejo* panels, is worth a visit.

Landscape and Crops
This is a large *freguesia* with diverse habitats. The dry cereal and grazing land of Castro Verde in the north gives way to deep valleys and high scrubland with scattered trees in the south. Few cereals are grown in the south as the soil is too stony and the land inclinations too steep, but sheep and goats are grazed on the hillsides, which are covered with Gum Cistus, Tree Heather, Green and French Lavender, and Honeysuckle-clad Strawberry Trees. The Strawberry Tree flowers with small clusters of creamy, waxy blossoms in late autumn, at the same time as the round red fruit from the previous year matures. Its extremely hard wood is used extensively for carving, notably for traditional spoons.

Fauna, Flora and Birdlife
Butterflies are numerous during spring and early summer in this floristically colourful area with alternating deep dark valleys and high plateaus which give extensive vistas. The colourful Spanish Festoon is usually the first to appear, usually near areas containing Birthwort, on which the larvae feed. The Cleopatra and Clouded Yellow, Large and Bath Whites quickly follow. The Spanish Marbled White and Woodland Grayling fly amongst the trees, under whose shady canopy Rabbits feed. White Storks wander through the fields, while Black and Red Kites fly overhead. The

A typical town house of the early 20th century with coloured tiles completely covering the exterior. These are seen throughout the south of the country, with small newer homes on the Algarve's south-east coast decorated in the same way.

43

Trithemis annulata is possibly one of the most beautiful dragonflies to be seen in this area, but rarely in the south. It is usually found near stagnant or running water. Other specialities are the Emperor, Golden-ringed and Migrant Hawker dragonflies.

Crested Larks with their pointed 'caps' forage on the overland tracks.

Crafts and Local Produce
The northern part of the *freguesia* is a gently undulating plain divided into large properties, where cereals grow and sheep graze on the extensive pasture, providing wool, meat and milk for cheese.

A busy artisans' workshop with eight weaving looms produces reasonably priced slip rugs, bathroom sets and bed covers using the offcuts from a northern T-shirt factory. They are of attractive designs, including the traditional diamond *montanhac* and the *espiga* (ear of wheat). As they are washable they make a practical buy. Adjoining the workshop is the shop, which sells articles and produce from the outlying regions, including typical woollen blankets with age-old designs, leather boots and shoes, pottery and lacework.

Close to the Parish Church is the 'Artesanato Beira Serra' craft shop. Not only does this sell products from the owner's village of São Barnabé (11), but also from throughout the Serra do Caldeirão region.

Almodôvar used to be well known for its cobblers. During the 1940s there were seventy families (men, women and children) all employed in this occupation, but now there are only three or four in the town and one or two in outlying villages.

José Luis Santos Lourenço buys his leather from further north near Santarem, and, working with his wife on an old Singer machine, he makes all manner of boots and shoes to order. Calf leather or the belly of cattle is cut out and machine-stitched flat, before being finished by hand. The

Almodôvar was traditionally renowned for its footwear. The cobblers' trade was a family business with father, mother and the children all playing their part in the 'production line'. With the arrival of modern techniques and materials, few craftsmen have managed to maintain their trade, with the result that hand-made shoes now command high prices.

heels are thicker, and the soles are made from two layers of leather. For stitching, nylon or thick linen threads are used.

On the town outskirts, António João Mendes and his son, Laurentino Coelho Mendes, produce fifty tons of honey annually. In early spring they take their 1,500 hives to the Algarve citrus orchards, and then in mid-season they move them to local maquis areas, where the bees collect from purple French Lavender and Green Lavender to produce the famous *rosmaninho* honey. The season's end sees them in areas around Beja where nectar is collected from sunflowers. This third type of honey crystallizes within fifteen days and is dark golden in colour. (Most of the crop is sold to Nestlé.) Honey collection is in June, July and August, with the third variety in September and October.

05 SANTA CRUZ

Santa Cruz *freguesia* is surrounded by Almodôvar (04) and São Barnabé (11) to the west, Ameixial (12) to the south, Martinlongo (13) and São Pedro de Solis (06) eastwards, with the remainder of Almodôvar (31) to the north. It is easily reached by taking a minor road eastwards from just south of Dogueno on the main Faro to Lisbon EN2.

Archaeology and Architecture
The village is situated above a valley to the south. Here, within the valley and completely hidden from above, is the magnificent Church of Santa Cruz, classified as a national monument. Beautifully positioned by a babbling stream, it has a magnificent Manueline portal and, further along within its grounds, a very small chapel lies at the water's edge.

Landscape and Crops
This *freguesia* slopes gently down to the Ribeira do Vascão, which forms its southern boundary. Small waterways flowing in from the flat, hard grain-growing land support abundant lush vegetation.

Fauna, Flora and Birdlife
The wooded valleys are full of birds, especially families of Long-tailed Tits, which are very different from the familiar bird seen in Northern Europe. Here they are very dark in colour, appearing almost black as they move rapidly amongst the foliage. Corn Buntings make their presence heard during the breeding season with their jangly song, but they are silent by July, although they can still be seen on wires and on cereal lands looking for grain.

Woodlarks are often seen amongst the scattered Cork Oak trees. These rather inconspicuous birds frequently sit on top

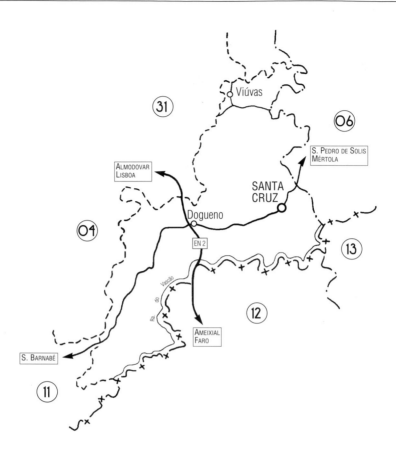

of a tree, lustily singing their distinctive and melodious notes. They are easily distinguished from the Short-toed Lark and Skylark (both of which are in the region) by the black and white mark at the elbow of the wing and the strong white eye stripe.

The Stonechat, another common bird found throughout these inland regions, likes to sit on top of a bush, thistle or fencing post in an open position – an ideal spot to scan the area for insects. The male is a pretty bird with a black head, white collar and reddish breast.

Sardinian and Dartford Warblers disappear low within the scrub cover, while during summer Montagu's Harriers quarter the open land, their place being taken in winter by the much less common Hen Harrier. In the river valleys where there is dense undergrowth, the diminutive Wren can more often be heard than seen, but quiet watching can reveal this tiny creature searching amongst the undergrowth.

Otters are still found all along the Ribeira do Vascão. This secretive mammal is often only detected by a gentle rippling in the water, but closer inspection may reveal footprints along the riverside.

Near the river an experimental unit has been established to breed and farm fish commercially. This has been helped by the Programme HORIZON in Denmark, which

This lovely Manueline doorway is at the magnificent Church of Santa Cruz which has recently been designated a national monument. Hidden away in a valley it is rarely seen or used, as a newer church has been constructed in the village, much higher up.

Below French Lavender is an extremely common constituent of garigue scrubland, and both this and the green variety are very high in nectar. Beehives are transported to these areas so that the bees can collect and produce the famous *rosmaninho* honey.

has sent personnel to assist with setting up the project. The fish being farmed are freshwater *achigas* (Big-mouthed Bass) and ornamental goldfish, the former for food – trying to break the Portuguese preference for salt-water fish – the latter for export.

In the village of Viúvas, within the grain and pasture land, a young farmer specializes in more unusual farm animals. He has a herd of Wild Boar and a herd of Belgian Pietrian pigs, all in brick-built sties. Besides keeping these two pure-

We came across this week-old orphan Wild Boar piglet in a local bar drinking warmed milk from a lemonade bottle with a baby's teat! The longitudinal golden stripes make it one of the most attractive young wild animals, but the parents can be extremely protective of their offspring.

bred herds, he also cross breeds to produce sucking-pig, a traditional and much loved dish in Southern Portugal. The hybrid between the domestic Pietrian and Wild Boar produces an incredibly beautiful little piglet, in which both parents' colours are passed on. Shining gold all over, it has black stripes on its flanks and black spots on its belly.

The farmer's other interests include a flock of Ile de France sheep, which are much larger than the traditional Merino type of the area, and goats, including breeding groups of Alpine, Grenadine and even Angora.

Crafts and Local Produce

The local population keeps traditional crafts going, with the barber doubling as a cobbler, and Dona Julieta using thick linen for crocheted table cloths and mats, as well as producing attractive knitwear. Traditional woven blankets and knitted socks are made using five needles rather than the conventional British four, and the bakery, as in so many of these inland *freguesias*, produces delicious bread. For art, Teresa Reis makes three dimensional pictures by placing three thick layers of paper within a frame over a silicone base. The paper is then cut into the desired shapes using a scalpel, and after painting the pictures are varnished. Bowls of flowers and ships in full sail are two of Teresa's specialities, and, of course, each work is unique.

06 SÃO PEDRO DE SOLIS, *07* SÃO MIGUEL DO PINHEIRO, *08* SÃO SEBASTIÃO DOS CARROS

The three *freguesias* of São Pedro de Solis, São Miguel do Pinheiro and São Sebastião dos Carros are best treated as one for the wildlife and geography, as they are very similar.

Landscape, Crops and Produce

Here, there are vast grain and pasture growing properties in a gently undulating countryside which rises up to 333m near São Pedro de Solis. Trees are few and far between, mainly Ilex Oak and a few eucalyptus, and provide the only shade for the thousands of sheep which are grazed in this region, one of the most important cheesemaking areas in southern Portugal. The small villages usually have some cultivated land nearby to supply vegetables to the community.

This White Stork nest is in a small Ilex Oak tree in the vast grain lands of the Alentejo. Storks nest in a variety of situations, including specially erected platforms, telephone poles, electricity pylons, chimneys, walls and church towers.

Fauna, Flora and Birdlife

Many of the large estates have been turned into hunting (shooting) reserves. These are securely fenced, and in many cases Red Deer populations have been established. Red-legged Partridge are reared and licences for small numbers of the protected Wild Boar provide adequate sport for visiting hunters.

An interesting project at Brites Gomes is Ostrich farming. These, the world's largest birds, are kept in extensive enclosures and fed on specially prepared food. They will eventually be used for meat and leather, but at the moment the production of breeding stock is the main object.

These *freguesias* are a riot of colour in spring and, as in the areas to the north (Castro Verde; 30, and Mértola; 32), the landscape is ever changing. Hillsides blanketed

with white daisies look as though they have a powdering of snow; Crown Daisies and *Gladiolus illyricus* grow unchecked by selective weed killers; and the ubiquitous *Cistus* species cover huge areas with large white flowers from March until late May. French and Green Lavender flourish, and the roadsides and areas between the rocks shine pink with the attractive low-growing *Cistus crispus*. Horned Dock also grows extensively, especially in the moist ground between trees in the orchards.

Thistles are a dominant feature of the local flora, and in some places they grow so thickly that the landscape becomes a riot of varying shades of pink and violet. Arguably most spectacular is the Cardoon, with its huge blue flower heads, which grows by the roadside.

In this vast open steppe land, Golden Eagles can sometimes be seen high in the sky riding on the thermals. Great and Little Bustards breed in the area and in season the jet black neck of the male Little Bustard can often be seen above the grain. This is also the stronghold for the Calandra Lark, the largest lark.

Crafts and Local Produce
Each area offers its own specialities. Crafts in particular have been carried down through the generations, and many ladies might work on a loom which once belonged to their maternal great grandmother. Throughout, the local history of all crafts seems to cease with great-grandparents, although one is led to believe that many are of more ancient origins.

The annual Horned Dock found under Ilex Oaks gives the countryside a reddish glow during spring and early summer. It grows predominantly on cultivated land under oaks, olive and fruit trees, and is named because of the teeth on its seed case.

06 SÃO PEDRO DE SOLIS

São Pedro de Solis is bordered to the north by Almodôvar (31), to the east by São Miguel do Pinheiro (07), to the south by Martinlongo (13), and westwards by Santa Cruz (05). It is accessible by turning eastwards from the main EN2 Faro to Lisbon road just south of Dogueno.

Archaeology and Architecture
The pretty little local church lies well outside the village. It is about two hundred years old and, as a result of restoration, displays a mixture of styles and designs, primarily Gothic and Manueline. The clean, plain interior has wooden benches, and a wooden floor and roof.

Crafts and Local Produce
This is an industrious village, and two ladies in particular are known for their

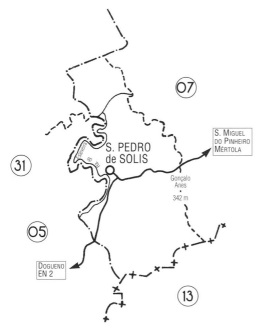

Blanket weaving is one of the crafts practised in the village. This very colourful example is on a cotton warp with a coloured wool weft. The loom originally belonged to the owner's maternal great grandmother and is typical of many found in these out-of-the-way hamlets.

craft work. Maria Teresa makes and sells pure woollen blankets using traditional patterns in natural or brown sheep wool. She also produces coloured blankets or ones made from rags, with smaller pieces in linen (*linho*) or cotton (*algodão*). Vitorinha Maria, meanwhile, makes attractive rag carpets and bedside rugs, as well as beautiful crocheted shawls and woollen socks knitted on five needles.

07 SÃO MIGUEL DO PINHEIRO

São Miguel do Pinheiro is bounded by Castro Verde (30) and São Pedro de Solis (06) to the west, Mértola (32) to the northeast, São Sebastião dos Carros (08) eastwards, and Martinlongo (13) to the south. It is reasonably easy to locate by taking the minor road which is signposted from the main EN267 from Almodôvar to Mértola.

Archaeology and Architecture
Between São Miguel do Pinheiro and Alcaria Longa, a hill site has vestiges of the Arab occupation. In the surrounding countryside, as in so many of these remote areas, a number of stone sheep corrals are in a reasonable state of preservation.

Perhaps one of the most beautiful churches in this region is the tiny, 250-year-old Igreja de Nossa Senhora de Santa Ana in Montes Santana, a hamlet of six houses in the south of the *freguesia*. Unmarked on many maps, Montes Santana is situated between the villages of Corcha and Roncão and can be reached by a hard-core track.

The interior of the church is completely decorated with well-preserved blue and white *azulejos* depicting biblical scenes. In the sacristy, a wall is devoted to wax and plaster ex-votos, a remnant of medieval culture more often seen in central Mediterranean areas. Tremendous local pride is attached to the church, and services are still conducted on certain days. Remember to sign the visitors' book, which is near to the offertory plate.

São Miguel do Pinheiro has a newly renovated windmill set within the village. This will be used as a tourist attraction, with bread ovens nearby and a restaurant serving typical food of the region. The original walls are approximately 1m thick, with the main millstone 130cm in diameter and weighing 900kg. The stone is of French origin and has already been there for 65 years. Prior to that

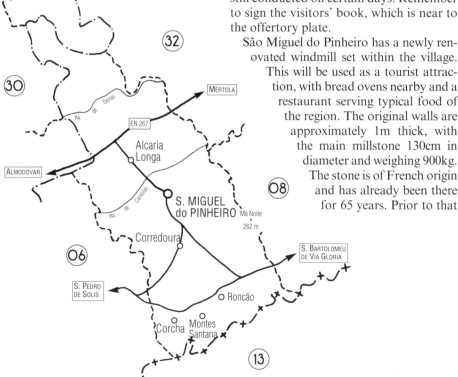

52

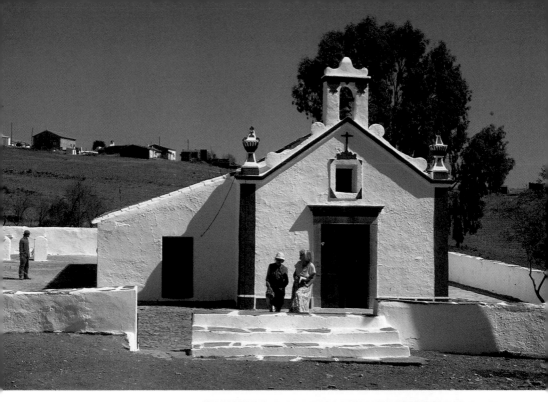

Above The nave in this tiny chapel at Montes Santana is approximately 8m long and completely covered with blue and white *azulejos* (tiles) which depict different biblical scenes. The small stone-built village is always bright from the annual lime-washing which keeps the cottages white.

This fine windmill has been restored with financial assistance from IN LOCO and the local council. Nearby, a new restaurant serves typical Alentejano food to order, but main meals are always available. Shortly new bread ovens will be in use to produce bread from the stone-ground flour.

A grain chute in the windmill channels cereals to two huge grinding stones which weigh 900kg each. These are turned by a simple set of gears which are revolved by the wind in the sails. When the wind blows and the mill is working, stone-ground flour should be for sale.

there was a Portuguese one, which had lasted for over 150 years.

The windmill roof revolves on a huge circular Ilex Oak rim which is supported on a series of small wheels, also made of Ilex, with the huge stout sail arm made of eucalyptus. Sails always face into the wind, with the earthenware cups on the spoke ends 'singing'. Any change in wind direction alters their tone, indicating the necessity to move the sail direction. Between 60kg and 80kg of maize or wheat are ground hourly (barley isn't ground as it is too fine).

Crafts and Local Produce
As in neighbouring Castro Verde (30), a number of younger people have been con-

tracted to make Arraiolos carpets. In Corredoura, meanwhile, a 12-year-old bakery produces 400 loaves daily, in ovens fired with pine and eucalyptus.

08 SÃO SEBASTIÃO DOS CARROS

São Sebastião dos Carros is bounded to the north by Mértola (32), to the east by Espírito Santo (09), southwards by Martinlongo (13) and Giões (14), and to the west by São Miguel do Pinheiro (07). It is fairly easily reached from the main EN267 Almodôvar to Mértola road, with many small interesting roads and tracks leading deep into the countryside.

During the winter, rain falls sparingly, but at times very heavy storms over the plains nourish the sprouting seeds. Here a rainbow is seen over the village of São Sebastião dos Carros, hopefully leaving its crock of gold for a bountiful golden harvest!

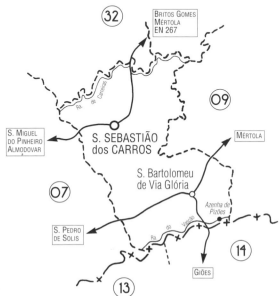

Local Produce

Although this is a small *freguesia* which historically has little to offer in comparison with its neighbours, it is home to one of the most important commodities within this Southern Alentejo province – sheep cheese, of the famous Serpa type. Between late September and the beginning of June, a daily average of 500 litres of ewe's milk is collected from the surrounding region between Mértola and Almodôvar. Cheese, sheep butter and curd cheeses (*requeijão*) are produced, in a process which requires careful control.

The Cardoon is a striking and common large thistle with great commercial importance. The stamens are collected and dried during the flowering season in early summer. Later an infusion is made from them to coagulate sheep and goats' milk for cheese (ideal for vegetarians!).

After boiling, the milk is cooled to hand temperature before adding salt and the coagulating agent. (The locally grown, indigenous Cardoon anthers and stigmas are dried and made into this very necessary infusion). After about 1½ hours the milk sets. It is then 'worked' by hand on a sloping board to express all the liquid, which is collected and later poured into a centrifuge for producing sheep butter. The semi-solid mass is used for the *requeijão*, or moulded and pressed into bottomless forms which are then removed and the cheeses wrapped with cloth to retain their shape. They are then placed on shelves to cure. The maturing takes from one to one and a half months. Naturally, while maturing the cheeses lose weight, but this important business sells approximately 50–70kg of cheese daily during the nine-month season.

09 ESPÍRITO SANTO

Espírito Santo is bounded to the east by the Guadiana river, which divides it from Spain, to the south by Giões (14), Pereiro (15) and Alcoutim (16), to the west by São Sebastião dos Carros (08), and to the north by Mértola *concelho* (32). It is accessible from the EN122 Vila Real de Santo

Cheese making. After coagulation the curds are pressed into forms and the liquid expressed, before curing for one to one and a half months. The liquid whey runs down the chute in the foreground to a large container, from which it goes to a centrifuge to be made into sheep butter.

António to Mértola eastern Algarve route, with several small tracks going into the surrounding countryside.

Archaeology and Architecture

The Parish Church, which dominates the *freguesia* capital of Espírito Santo, can be seen from kilometres away and is of Roman and Arabic origin. Its wooden interior dates from the 14th century; the keys for visiting are kept at the Post Office.

The small village of Mesquita shows its Arabic origins, its name meaning 'mosque'.

A quaint 20th-century 'memorial' can be found on the banks of the Rio Guadiana opposite Pomarão. This is reached by passing through the village of Mesquita and continuing along the hard-core track to the river. Here there are several derelict buildings, which were once the offices and warehouses of a ship's chandler, who used to provide provisions for the boats which transported copper ore from Pomarão to Vila Real de Santo António (ore which had been sent from Mina de São Domingos by rail). A large dovecote also remains, and has two very fine *azulejo* panels covering part of the walls, erected by J. Abecasis, civil engineer for Mason and Barry, in 1926. Depicted are the owners from the past century, John Laurence Danino (owner from 1864 to 1885) and Henry Joseph Danino (1868–1879).

Landscape and Crops

Shallow-soiled rolling cereal and pasture land typifies this *freguesia*, with the undulating grassland very hot in summer and cold in winter. Few trees grow to shelter the large flocks of sheep, except near the Rio Guadiana and its tributary the Ribeira do Vascão, which forms the southern boundary of the Alentejo. Bamboo grows in profusion near the moist banks of these water courses, providing raw material for basket making.

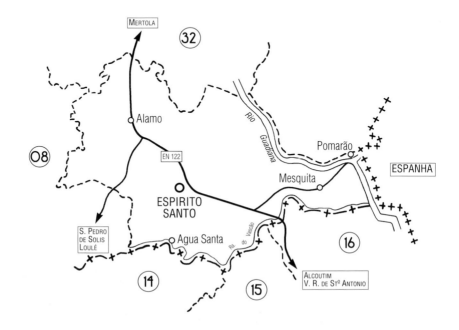

Above The magnificent Igreja Matriz (Parish Church) of Espírito Santo stands in a prominent position, with parts dating back to Roman times. This small village – like so many – suffers from an exodus of the younger generation who have left to find more lucrative jobs abroad or on the coastal tourist strip.

Fauna, Flora and Birdlife

Around the small declining villages, vegetables and fruit are grown and many ruined windmills are now used as nesting sites by countless White Storks. Thousands of wintering Golden Plover feed on insects and green matter. Calandra and Thekla Larks are common throughout the year, with Montagu's Harriers quartering the land during the summer in search of food.

In a remote area on the Guadiana river bank opposite the village of Pomarão lie the ruins of a ship's chandler, which serviced boats transporting copper ore from São Domingos. The dovecote here was erected in 1926 to the memory of the Danino brothers, who were responsible for revictualling the boats.

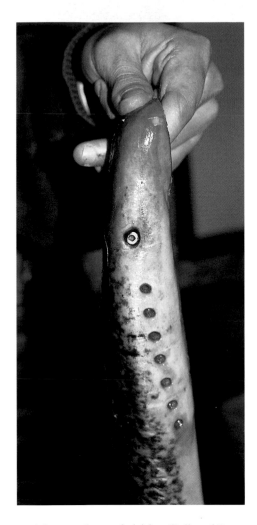

The boneless Lamprey swims upriver to spawn. Considered a culinary delicacy throughout Portugal, it commands high prices. This primitive creature has a sucker-like mouth for attaching itself to, and for consuming, decaying animal matter in slow-flowing water courses.

A large colony of visiting Collared Pratincoles is now established in a small remote lake, and can frequently be seen in summer hunting for insects.

In the Casa Verde restaurant on the EN122 at Espírito Santo, there is a room full of stuffed mammals which were shot in this area. This practice is now prohibited, but it is interesting to see the display, which includes Egyptian Mongoose, Wild Boar and Red Fox, plus an enormous Ocellated Lizard skin measuring 1.25m in length!

Out in the countryside Genet, Wild Cat, Beech Marten and Badger are found, as are Otters in the river banks.

The rivers sustain several kinds of freshwater fish, eels and the valuable Lamprey.

In terms of flora, this grazing land is beautiful in spring, with huge expanses of Corn Marigold and Crown Daisy, Vipers Bugloss and Catchfly. Agua Santa on the Ribeira do Vascão is a delightful spot, with its banks covered with Oleanders. Here there are some medicinal sulphurous wells and a bath house where hot baths are still taken for a variety of ailments (details from the Casa Verde restaurant).

Dragonflies can be seen patrolling their territories, notably the Beautiful Demoiselle, which is almost black with navy blue wings, and the uncommon *Trithemis annulata*, which is dark red with a purple powdery covering in the male.

Crafts and Local Produce
In terms of crafts, the area is home to one artisan of exceptional note. In the small hamlet of Alamo, besides a man who makes the donkey saddles (*albardas*) and collars (*molins*), there is probably the only tanner in the region. Curing mainly sheep, goat, Wild Boar and Red Fox skins, Venceslau Sequeira Luis soaks them for several days in a salt solution and then scrapes them to remove the fat. They are washed with soap and water and dried in the sun on a home-made frame which looks rather like a kite. It takes a week to comb out the matted coat on the soft, pliable, leather sheep skins, but the final product is beautiful, soft, white wool.

10 SÃO MARCOS DA SERRA

São Marcos da Serra is bordered to the north by Santana da Serra (01), to the east by São Barnabé (11), to the south by São Bartolomeu de Messines (17) and Silves (35), and to the west by Monchique (34) and Odemira (28). It is well situated on the main highway E01 from Seville to Vigo via Faro, Lisbon and Porto, with a projected road to Monchique well under way.

Archaeology and Architecture
This typical small town within the northern area of the Algarve is perched on top of a high ridge, with fascinating, winding, steep streets and excellent views over the surrounding countryside. The ancient Parish Church of São Marcos (St. Mark

the Evangelist) is well preserved and has recently been renovated. It occupies the highest point in the town and has strong, protective walls, hence its traditional name, 'The Castle'.

Landscape and Crops
The basic underlying rock of this area is Carboniferous slate and shale which is impervious to water, and therefore there is considerable erosion. The Ribeira de Ode-louca runs through the *freguesia*, and in the river valley and its tributaries wheat and maize grow in the fertile soil, as well as vegetables for local consumption, oranges and other fruit.

Fauna, Flora and Birdlife
Pigs forage underneath the oak trees for acorns, which constitute their main item of

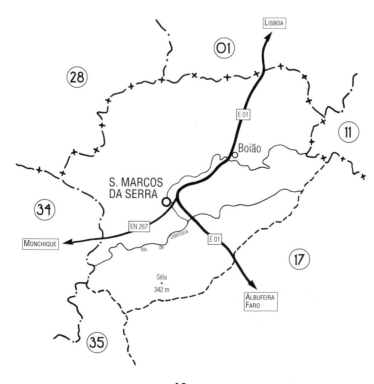

Some remarkably large Ilex Oak grow in this area. Usually flat topped, they are pruned periodically for charcoal and for encouraging acorn production. Acorns are not only fed on by pigs, but are also roasted for human consumption. The trees are vital for sheltering domestic animals.

food in the autumn. The forestry industry, in the form of terraced hillsides planted with Maritime Pine and Eucalyptus, is extensive.

Cork and Ilex Oak are indigenous. Near Boião a huge Ilex Oak with a crown of 28.5m in diameter was destroyed a few years ago due to decay, but there are still numbers of very large specimens in the area.

Eucalyptus is pollarded every ten years for wood pulp. After the first cutting, two or three of the strongest dormant basal buds are allowed to grow, producing a further cut nine to ten years later. This procedure is continued for about four cuts, after which the ground is completely devoid of any nutrients. The trees are then grubbed out and the hillsides allowed to revert to natural scrub once again.

The large white flowers of the Gum Cistus have five petals, each with a maroon spot at the base. The Narrow-leaved and Salvia-leaved Cistus are smaller, as are their pure white flowers. The Grey-leaved Cistus with beautiful pale pink flowers is in bloom from March to May, while the low-growing, bright pink *Cistus crispus* carpets the ground near the road edges. The overall effect is a colourful picture.

Thanks to the locally well-known São Marcos Depression, which divides the Serra de Monchique from the Serra do Caldeirão and through which the main Lisbon road and railway run, birds are numerous and can easily be seen from the roadsides. Along the Odelouca river the Grey Wagtail, with its lemon-yellow

Left *Centaurium erythraea* subspecies *grandiflorum* is a very common flowering plant of the scrubland during the early summer months. It is also extremely variable in colour, ranging from almost white to a deep shocking pink.

Right *Chouriça* is a traditional pig product which when added to casseroles gives a distinctive flavour due to the smoking, the sweet red peppers and the garlic paste. It is also an ingredient of *feijoada*, a traditional pork and dried bean casserole.

Crafts and Local Produce

Within the town, furniture is made from bamboo. As in the surrounding districts, weaving, patchwork and other crafts are carried out in local homes.

Visiting the local exhibitions, it becomes clear that within this well-wooded *freguesia* with its outlying scrublands, honey, *medronho* and all the associated commodities are produced, including honey cakes and many other confections.

Four bakeries provide for the town and the surrounding areas, and local specialities include salted ham (*presunto*), smoked *chouriça*, *lingüiça* and *paio*.

In rural areas there is hardly a home without its family pig. These are usually black in colour, shorter and very much fatter than their North European counterparts. During spring and summer they are fed on household scraps, but towards autumn, which is the traditional slaughtering time, they are fattened on maize and figs which are unfit for human consumption, and also on acorns from the Cork and Ilex Oaks, which impart an exquisite flavour to the meat.

The slaughter of the family pig is almost ritualistic and calls for a party. The men butcher and prepare the carcass, while the women deal with the meat, making *chouriça* and other preserves for the forthcoming year. These are usually smoked and cured in the vast chimneys.

underparts and grey back, can usually be spotted. An occasional Kingfisher streaks up the river like a sapphire arrow, emitting its unmistakable piercing whistle. In early summer, Nightingales sing in the valley and Woodchat Shrikes sit on vantage points, often dead trees, looking for prey. Jays are common in the woods and are easily identified by their striking white rumps.

Butterflies similar to those found in the neighbouring *freguesia* of São Barnabé (11) are numerous during the spring. The Spanish Festoon, a very spectacular one found in both locations, is closely related to but much smaller than the Swallowtail. It has a base colour of buff and yellow, strong black markings and a number of red spots on both upper and lower wings. It can be seen only in the early part of the year, as it has just one brood feeding on Birthwort.

Nova (03) to the north, and Almodôvar (04) and Santa Cruz (05) eastwards. It is reached by small roads from either Almodôvar or Dogueno on the main Faro to Almodôvar EN2 road, or from just north of São Marcos da Serra, off the main IP1 highway (turn east past Boião and go through the village of Vale de Hortas, where a small bridge crosses the River Odelouca). Several small roads lead from the Algarve, including that from Salir to Sitio das Éguas via Malhão. Until recently, São Barnabé was difficult to reach, and as a result the hamlets of this quaint *freguesia* seem lost in time.

Archaeology and Architecture

The tiny church in Santa Susana is currently being renovated, while the one in São Barnabé was restored

Fat is rendered down for lard. In the evening when most of the initial chores are finished, a feast is eaten, washed down with vast quantities of red wine. The following day completes the work, giving occasion for further revelry.

in 1963. The latter is simple inside, with marble floors, a plain nave and ceiling, and wooden benches. São Barnabé, the 'Santo da Terra' (Patron Saint) of the small community, looks down over the altar from his gilded wooden throne.

11 SÃO BARNABÉ

São Barnabé is surrounded by Santana da Serra (01) and São Marcos da Serra (10) to the west, São Bartolomeu de Messines (17), Alte (18) and Salir (20) to the south, Gomes Aires (02) and Santa-Clara-a-

Many of the houses within São Barnabé are 200–300 years old. They are mostly built on 'terraces' on the hillsides above the sloping roads, and are reached by steps which lead to the hewn slate paving slabs which form the pathways. Often without windows, the houses are low buildings with thick adobe walls and roofs covered with boards inside and tiles on the outside.

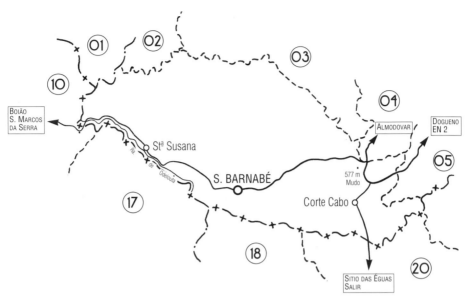

Landscape and Crops

The *freguesia* is divided from the Algarve by the Ribeira de Odelouca, which cuts through the hard Carboniferous slate of the area to join the Ribeira de Arade just north of Estômbar, before reaching the ocean at Portimão.

The steep hillsides, which rise to 577m at Mudo, have a few laboriously tilled cereal patches, but are mostly covered by Cork Oak woods with an undergrowth of cistus, some large *Viburnum tinus*, and the Strawberry Tree, from whose ripe fruits *medronho* is distilled. Together with cork collection, this is the economic mainstay of the region.

Immediately to the north of Mudo is the source of the Rio Mira which enters the sea on the west coast, while to the east of Mudo is the source of the Riberia de Oeiras which enters the Rio Guadiana at Mértola.

A flock of Campaniça sheep grazing amongst Ilex Oaks, with the Alentejo plains in the far background. Lamb production normally takes place from the end of September, just before the rainy season which should bring succulent new grass.

Fauna, Flora and Birdlife

Plantations of Maritime Pine and Eucalyptus have recently been established, mainly for the wood pulp industry. In the valleys near Santa Susana and São Barnabé, fertile vegetable crops are neatly tended to sustain the dwindling population. A few goats graze the hillsides, providing milk, cheese and meat, while bees produce delicious honey from the mountain flowers.

Rabbits and Red Foxes are relatively common, the Rabbits being hunted for food during winter months.

Right The common but beautiful Grape Hyacinth is found in all habitats except salt marshes. It can easily be confused with the much rarer *Bellevalia hackelii*, but the latter has looser flower spikes and is more mauve in colour.

Wild Boar, Genet and Egyptian Mongoose are also common, but the first two are rarely seen. These are protected and a licence must be obtained for culling Wild Boar if population control becomes necessary.

Birds within the cork woods are numerous, and include quantities of Azure-winged Magpies, Jays, Bee-eaters, woodpeckers, Great Grey Shrikes, Short-toed Treecreepers and Nuthatches. Smaller birds such as Sardinian and Dartford Warblers, various tits, Stonechat and Corn Bunting are easily seen in scrub areas.

The Two-tailed Pasha butterfly is common during May–June and September wherever large numbers of Strawberry Trees grow. The second brood come from the influx of migrant butterflies earlier in the year. Other butterflies commonly found are the Swallowtail, Speckled Wood, Wood White, many of the blues, Cleopatra and Clouded Yellow, and the Green Hairstreak, especially during the spring.

Crafts and Local Produce

São Barnabé has its own *Cooperativa de Artesanato*, an artisans' cooperative group working mainly within local homes. Products are sold in special exhibitions which are held throughout the area, or at *Artesanato Beira Serra*, which can be found near the church in Almodôvar (04) and which is owned and run by the cooperative's president.

The area is renowned for its patchwork, many excellent examples of which are made in the village, including cushion covers in varying designs, oven gloves, bags and bedspreads.

This village is renowned for its patchwork, and like many other areas produces some exceptionally good work. This lady is sitting outside her tiny cottage, a home approached by steep steps and an uneven slab pavement. Note the Roman-type tiles and the lack of windows.

The material, after being cut into the desired shapes, is ironed and then machined into place by an old hand-operated sewing machine. A simple cushion cover takes around one day to complete, with more elaborate designs requiring longer.

Unsophisticated rag dolls portray local traditions and characters. The shepherd is shown with his sheep, and donkeys and windmills also feature.

Beautiful crochet work, including very realistic carnations, is another speciality of this small community, and the ladies from this *freguesia* will shortly be producing dried flower arrangements as well.

Medronho, with its own special label, is another product which is fast becoming recognized. Conforming to the latest regulations, it is made between October and December after harvesting the fruit from the Strawberry Tree in late autumn.

Excellent honey originates from the large tracts of natural vegetation which are untouched by artificial fertilizers or pesticides.

12 AMEIXIAL

Ameixial is bounded to the north-west by Santa Cruz (05), to the west by Martinlongo (13) and Cachopo (21), and to the south by Salir (20). It is easily accessible from the EN2 (once the main route to the Algarve from Lisbon), with a minor road to Martinlongo and Cachopo.

Archaeology and Architecture

Well marked and leading off the Martinlongo and Cachopo road is the Anta da Pedra do Alagar, a 4000-year-old Neolithic dolmen (walking is advised when the road begins to deteriorate). Further along one is directed to the Azenha do Pisão, a 19th-century river mill situated in picturesque surroundings. The first part of the route is easily driven, but walking is again advised at the last turn near the bridge by the river.

Within this remote area at Corte de Ouro there are many round Celtic-type homes. These dwellings, 4m in diameter and now used as cereal stores, are made of heavy hewn schist stone with thatched roofs. Only 150 years ago they were still used as homes.

This identical style of circular building is found from the Shetland Islands in the northern parts of the United Kingdom, through western Ireland, into Galicia in northern Spain and south into the north of Portugal. It is likely that they are of Celtic origin, as the Moroccan Berber buildings of this era are either square or rectangular.

Landscape and Crops

The highest point in this *freguesia* is on the EN2 at the Miradouro do Caldeirão

(545m). From here the views are spectacular – the *serras* look like a petrified boiling cauldron (*caldeirão*) with the hard Carboniferous slate eroded into rounded, smooth-topped hills. The poor, shallow soil is used for cereal growing, and the hills are so steep that most cultivation is either by mule or by hand, with all harvesting done by hand. The simple crop rotation in these remote hills is wheat followed by oats, and then two or three years' fallow before the rotation starts again. Sometimes sheep manure is spread, but this is scarce and is usually used on vegetable crops nearer to the villages. Harvesting is by sickle (made in Cachopo by the only sickle-maker south of Lisbon!), with men and women working side by side under the hot sun, their fingers covered with fitted

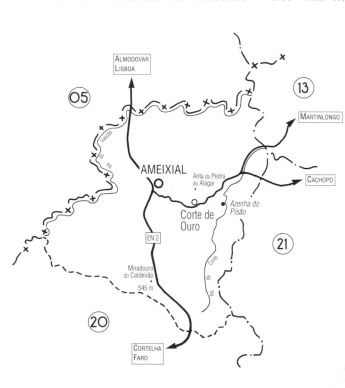

bamboo sleeves (*canudos*) for protection. When the sheaves are fully dry they are transported to a mobile threshing drum at a communal plot.

Fauna, Flora and Birdlife

River valleys are usually bordered by Oleanders, which, when in full flower in June, make an unforgettable sight. Also unforgettable is the fact that this plant is very poisonous, with one leaf containing enough poison to kill a person!

In other areas Eucalyptus is grown for wood pulp and around the small villages vegetable crops for home consumption. Cork is an important economic crop, being carefully stripped once every nine to eleven years depending on the thickness. The number on the trunk of the cork trees is the final digit of the year in which it was last cut.

The Gum Cistus scrub, which can reach 1–1.5m high, is also 'harvested' and, after being left to dry, bundled and taken to the villages to be used as fuel for the bread ovens. Once the cistus is cut, regeneration quickly takes place, with a multitude of annual plants forming a cover for French

Having a well-earned rest. Cutting cereals with a sickle on these steep hillsides is tiring and back-breaking work, especially in the relentless sun. Men and women usually work together (the women with a smaller sickle) cutting and binding cereals into sheaves before stacking them in heaps.

Lavender and more cistus. The flowers provide nectar for the many beehives scattered in the hillsides, and eventually end up as some of the world's finest honey.

Crafts and Local Produce

Beeswax is used for top-grade floor or furniture polish and ecclesiastical candles. It is also good for preserving saddlery and keeping fishing lines pliable, amongst numerous other uses.

In Cortelha, in addition to buying wax from throughout the Algarve and Alentejo, one beeswax producer has at least 100 hives of his own. After the honey is extracted from the combs, the wax is steamed three times to remove impurities. It is then poured into moulds to form 11kg blocks, suitable for transporting or exporting, or used for making the wax foundations for filling supers for hives.

The industrious ladies of Ameixial village work hard in their own homes to make rag dolls dressed in regional costume and depicting country life. (The production of these dolls is described under the *freguesia* of Querença, 25.) The dolls are currently sold at various exhibitions and in Serra Mae 'Casa da Serra' shops in Salir, Loulé and Faro, but in future they may also be available in the village itself if plans for a campsite, games area and shop go ahead.

The proposed location for the campsite is at the entrance to the Martinlongo–Cachopo road, just past the cemetery with its skull and crossbones on the iron gates. This will make a particularly good base for visiting the surrounding regions from São Marcos da Serra (10) to Almodôvar (04), Cachopo (21), Espírito Santo (09), and Alcoutim (16).

Rag dolls are still made in many small villages and were at one time much treasured possessions of the young children. Now, these traditionally dressed dolls have become a saleable product and here in Ameixial a group of younger women work diligently to produce them.

13 MARTINLONGO

Martinlongo is bounded to the north by São Pedro de Solis (06), São Miguel de Pinheiro (07) and São Sebastião dos Carros (08), to the east by Giões (14), to the south by Vaqueiros (22) and Cachopo (21), and to the west by Ameixial (12) and Santa Cruz (05). It is centrally placed on the EN124 Barranco do Velho to Alcoutim road, with minor routes southwards to Vaqueiros and westwards to Ameixial.

Archaeology and Architecture
If you travel to the south-east of this *freguesia*, an interesting walk goes from Santa Justa to the ruins of the Roman castle at Cerro do Castelo on top of a hill 2km away. The climb is not too steep and there are magnificent views from the top – it is obvious why a castle was built in this strategic position.

Martinlongo's Parish Church has some Gothic and 17th-century features and is impressively adorned with a White Stork's nest on its tower!

Landscape and Crops
The highest point within this *freguesia* is Pereirão (353m), where there is a windmill as is usual on most high points. The bedrock is slate and schist, but thanks to higher rainfall than the *freguesias* to the north and east, it can sustain more vegetation. Pasture land in the north offers grazing for goats and sheep, but cereals are grown on the steep hillsides near the Foupana river, and these demand harvesting by hand. A few Eucalyptus plantations have been established for timber production in remote areas which offer no other viable economic use. Many of the higher slopes are covered with tall cistus scrub which is periodically cut for fuelling the family bread ovens. This can be seen drying

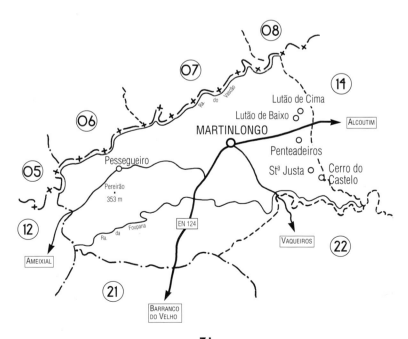

The sparse crops on the stony hillsides are cut by sickles which are still hand-made locally. This is a very skilled craft as the blade needs to be carefully serrated to make sure it keeps sharp. The reapers wear cane finger stalls called *canudos* for protection.

in bundles on hillsides or within the villages, where it remains for at least a year.

Fauna, Flora and Birdlife

The bridge over the Foupana river is a nesting site for Crag Martins, House Martins, and Red-rumped Swallows, which build a strange flask-shaped nest with a tube for an entrance. Golden Orioles, Azure-winged Magpies, Kingfishers, Great Spotted Woodpeckers and Little Ringed Plovers can often be seen on the verdant river banks.

Rabbits, Egyptian Mongoose, Wild Boar and Red Fox are all present, and the former two can often be seen during the daytime.

Crafts and Local Produce

One business which began in 1985 in this remote village and now has 28 mainly women employees is the only private bakery which exports to Spain – its 'bread round' runs from Sanlúcar de Guadiana in Spain to Ayamonte, Vila Real de Santo António and back to Alcoutim!

In a small garage in the village one man has amassed an incredible collection of miniature animals and figures which he makes from old branches and roots. The Cork Oak snakes and lizards are a particularly impressive part of the collection.

Mating Long-tailed Blues. Although the underside of the wing is mottled in pale brown with two coloured spots, the upperwing is bright blue. A very fast flyer, it is strongly migratory, often reaching Britain from the Mediterranean, where the larvae feed within the pods of Leguminosae.

Swallowtail butterflies are usually found in the Fennel by the roadsides, since this is the larvae food plant. The brilliant yellow Cleopatra, with an orange patch on the fore wing, is more common during early summer. The blues are numerous, especially in grasslands, as well as the Small Copper, Spanish Gatekeeper, Large White, Speckled Wood and the colourful Spanish Festoon.

Sheep and goats, the main domestic animals, are used for meat and milk production, while their high-quality wool is spun in the local cottages.

Elsewhere in the village, a group of local women have established a dolls workshop called 'A Flor da Agulha'. No fewer than 36 different dolls can be seen – and bought – at their tiny blue and white, three-roomed cottage. The dolls are (to quote from their brochure) 'leaving the village so that they can remain'. They depict old village characters, woodmen and shepherds, ladies cutting cereals, and traditional activities such as bringing in firewood, bread making, spinning, crocheting and many more.

The production of these 20cm miniatures is complex. The basic shape is formed from wire, thickly bound with sticky tape, after which a jute padding is stitched into place to produce the naked form. (The jute is now imported from Scotland!) Linen thread is stitched to the head to form hair, which is variously styled according to the character depicted. This slightly paler linen contrasts with the main material.

Most of the clothing is made from jute, with jute thread knitted to form shawls for elderly ladies. Aprons and scarves come in various coloured cottons, while baskets and hats are made from woven palm leaf (the local Dwarf Fan Palm) by specialists in Estômbar, Lagoa (39). The figurines are finally shaped into realistic positions.

Organically produced herbs are grown on a 1.5ha plot nearby, all wired in to

These jute dolls have become very popular, and over 30 different ones are produced. Besides the popular nativity they include figures doing everything from collecting the newly sheared wool to knitting it! Village life is illustrated by women who are bread making or doing crochet or tatting work; men are depicted as shepherds or woodmen.

protect it from sheep, goats and Wild Boar. The herbs are grown without pesticides or artificial chemicals; sheep manure is used for fertilizer, and irrigation is carried out when necessary. Seeds sown during February and March are usually harvested and dried before the heat of the summer damages them. Drying takes approximately two days and is done in a shed fanned by a through-draught of hot air, which is achieved by a low zinc-covered air duct heated by the sun.

A Companhia das Ervas produces twelve different herbs, attractively packed and labelled with a number from the Portuguese Association of Biological Agriculture which guarantees authenticity. Lemon Grass, *Erva ursa*, Balm, Lemon Verbena, Marigold, Peppermint, Penny Royal, Rosemary, Sage, Algerian Tea, Sweet Bay and Sweet Basil are their specialities, and they can be obtained from their restaurant headquarters, *Monte Branco*.

In the village of Lutão de Baixo, Benvinda Maria da Costa makes lovely dried flowers using the sheaths from maize cobs. The anthers and stems are made from green plastic wire, around which each piece of dried foliage is bound into place with nylon thread, the first ones curving inwards, the outer petals recurved, the final result looking like a huge chrysanthemum. Single flowers or basket arrangements are available. Her husband makes the baskets, as well as attractive wide-brimmed hats.

In Lutão de Cima, Rogério Guerreiro makes miniatures from whittled wood: birds and painted objects, as well as fascinating baskets from a single almond shell and a series of entwined rings from a single piece of wood. In the same hamlet, Catarina Maria Fernandes works with cotton to produce wonderful crocheted tablecloths and mats.

West of Martinlongo, in Pessegueiro, Virgílio do Rosário is a tinsmith – a craft which has fast disappeared during the last 20 years. He makes buckets, measuring utensils and other necessities.

In the tiny hamlet of Penteadeiros, with its quaint, low built, lichen-covered houses, Maria Senhorinha weaves beautiful fabrics out of linen, cotton and wool. Her loom and spinning wheel are well-used antiques of extremely rustic design. Her husband, Manuel Domingos, crushes raw flax with a home-made contraption made from Ilex Oak. The flax is first soaked in water for approximately nine days to rot the outer skin and then dried in the sun. After breaking the outer coat it is combed and spun, and then whitened by boiling it with Oleander ash before drying in the sun again 'until it smells very good'. It is then ready for use.

14 GIÕES AND *15* PEREIRO

As both these *freguesias* fall into the same geographical region, they can initially be dealt with together.

Landscape and Crops
Giões and Pereiro lie on a high tableland of hard rock covered mainly with Gum and Narrow-leaved Cistus, especially near the Alentejo border. Few cereal crops are grown, but, where the scrub has been cleared, grassland has been established, providing food for large flocks of sheep. Many stone sheep corrals are still used for sorting stock, but no longer for protection against predators.

Fauna, Flora and Birdlife
Oleander is native to the area and grows profusely at the Ribeira do Vascão. It makes a colourful sight in June and July, when its large, single, pink flowers belie its poisonous leaves.

During springtime, the roadsides are often covered with the Barbary Nut (*Iris*

sisyrinchium), a beautiful, variably coloured, blue-flowered plant whose blooms
open in full sun during the afternoon.

Along the roadsides Great Grey Shrikes
perch on telegraph lines, and are joined in
summer by Woodchat Shrikes and Bee-
eaters, all watching for insects from this
good vantage point.

Short-toed Eagles and sometimes even
Golden Eagles may occasionally be seen
high overhead, on the look-out for larger
prey. Dartford and Sardinian Warblers
hunt in the scrubland, while Golden Ori-
ole, Azure-winged Magpie, Kingfisher and
Nightingale are often found on the river
banks, with Common Sandpipers on the
shore line. During the migration seasons
countless birds stop to quench their thirst.

Rabbits and Brown Hares are frequently
seen, but Wild Boar, which is also common
in the area, is mainly nocturnal and hides in
the river valleys during the daytime.

The Clouded Yellow, Small Copper and
Speckled Wood butterflies are abundant
during the spring.

This *Argiope lobata* is common in all
parts of southern Portugal and
makes its intricate orb web in
gardens or scrubland. It looks
fearsome and aggressive but is
perfectly harmless. This family is
easily recognized by the peculiar
thick, corkscrew-like thread from
the centre of the web. The
picture shows the remains of the
eaten male!

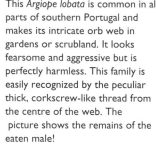

The low-growing *Cistus crispus* is
one more of the delightful shrubs
which flourishes in southern Portugal. This one is embellished with an
attractive metallic green beetle
which is common on the flowers of
Cistus and the related yellow or
white *Helianthemum* species.

By the Ribeira do Vascão, the attractive red dragonfly with its purple pruinescence, *Trithemis annulata*, can be seen, as well as the blue Keeled Skimmer and the much larger Emperor Dragonfly. The Ruddy Darter is extremely common, as are a number of blue damselflies belonging to the *Ischnura* group.

It is not uncommon to see water snakes, Viperine and Grass, gliding effortlessly through the water, feeding on tadpoles, adult Marsh Frogs and small fish.

14 GIÕES

Giões lies at the northern extremity of the Algarve and is bounded to the north by Espírito Santo (09) and São Sebastião dos Carros (08) in the Baixo Alentejo, to the east by Pereiro (15) in the Algarve, to the south by Vaqueiros (22), and to the west by Martinlongo (13). It is situated on a small road which joins Mértola with the Silves to Alcoutim EN124 major road, and other minor roads radiating into the countryside.

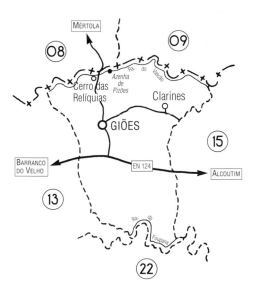

Archaeology and Architecture

Within this parish there are vestiges of a Roman fort at Cerro das Reliquias near the Ribeira do Vascão, and several stone sheep corrals. The latter were originally introduced as a way of 'folding' the sheep at night to protect them from wolves, which were prevalent here up until the beginning of the 20th century. In many cases a small covered stone dwelling is incorporated and was used by the shepherds, who stayed with their flocks day and night.

On the river banks there are ruins of several river mills, one or two of which have been restored. These work on a similar principle to tidal mills, with water diverted through a channel when the river is in full flow, powering turbines which, by a series of cogs, work the millstones.

After crossing the Ribeira do Vascão, there is a pretty walk along the northern bank, heading eastwards past the old mill. Where the river widens at one of the restored mills there are breathtaking views.

The attractive little Parish Church is set within a large square at the highest point in the village and can plainly be seen on the approach from the south. It houses various artefacts from the 16th and 17th centuries.

Crafts and Local Produce

At the northern end of the village, on the road to the Ribeira do Vascão and Baixo Alentejo, António Joaquim makes large, heavy baskets from the bamboo which he collects from the river banks. These are used either for potato picking or for carrying clothes to the communal washing house, which lies at the southern entrance to the village. If the canes are old and dry they are soaked in water for three days to soften them.

Traditional rustic cottage chairs are also constructed here, as well as typical baskets from the grass known as *palhinha* (*see* Vaqueiros, 22).

Goats forage on the surrounding hillsides, and during spring and summer their milk is used for making cheese.

As in many neighbouring *freguesias*, weaving from sheep wool, linen and cotton takes places in the hamlet of Clarines.

Traditional saddlery is still carried out for items such as a *molim*, the ornate, inverted V-shaped heavy collar worn by mules when pulling carts. (Carts here are pulled entirely from the neck and shoulders, so a well-fitting collar is absolutely essential.) These are made of tightly bound rye straw covered with leather, while the inner surface has a covering of soft sheepskin. The upper surface, which holds the 'lyre-shaped' wood which supports the shafts of the cart, is usually made of durable Wild Boar (*javali*) leather. Initially, the collar is stitched into shape with the two different leathers being joined together. This is very arduous work, and requires a substantial leather protective 'glove' to be worn over the palm of the hand, with a heavy metal disc over the centre which is used for pushing the needles through the tough leather. Once the collar shape is acquired, the whole

15 PEREIRO

Pereiro is bounded by Espírito Santo (09) to the north, Alcoutim (16) to the east, Giões (14) to the west, and Vaqueiros (22) and Odeleite (23) to the south. It is situated on the EN124 from Barranco do Velho to Alcoutim, and is also accessible on a minor road which wends its way to Alcoutim.

Archaeology and Architecture
This is a really typical *freguesia* capital with long, straight, narrow streets, low white-washed houses with traditional pantile roofs, and an impressive church on the outskirts, which dominates the countryside.

Crafts and Local Produce
Wandering through the streets on a bright afternoon, you'll find the local ladies sitting outside their homes knitting socks and jumpers, or crocheting items such as cushion covers.

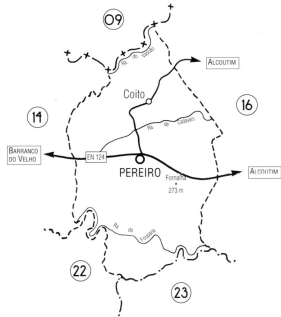

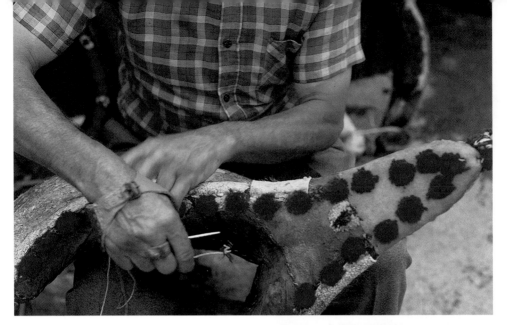

Here a mule collar is being repaired. The picture shows the usual woollen decoration which is so much a feature of these useful but ornate collars. Stitching is very tough work and hand protection needs to be worn for pushing the needle.

is stuffed with the rye straw and completed. Two round 'knobs' at the lower ends of the 'V' are where knotted ropes hold it together at the throat, making a snug fit and thus preventing rubbing on the mule's neck.

Traditionally, all collars are decorated with brightly coloured wool designs, bells and often a small mirror at the apex, and much of this decorative work also demands a lot of tough stitching.

Other industries in the village include making anchors for fishing boats, constructing circular frames for holding fishing nets and collecting cockles on the coastline, and putting together spears for

In many of the more remote villages the women sit outside their cottages doing their knitting or crochet work. Here Madge (third from right) chats with a group in the main thoroughfare, and admires their knitted pan holders.

catching lampreys in the river. Mattocks (*enxadãos*) are also made here – both the normal solid ones and others with two prongs – as well as branding irons and a variety of farm implements and tools.

16 ALCOUTIM

Alcoutim is divided from Spain to the east by the Guadiana River, and is bounded by Espírito Santo (09) to the north, Pereiro (15) to the west and Odeleite (23) southwards. It has three access roads, two of which join the Mértola to Vila Real de Santo António EN122 road, and another which follows the river down to Foz de Odeleite.

Rarely visited by tourists, this beautiful old Roman town with its winding cobbled streets, once known as *Alcoutinium,* was an important port during the time of the Phoenicians, Greeks and Carthaginians. It was also occupied by the Arabs from the 8th to the 13th centuries.

Archaeology and Architecture
Prehistoric and Roman remains are continually being discovered in the area, making it difficult to say exactly from when the town's dominating ruined castle dates. The building is thought to be pre-Arab, and it is certain that restoration work was carried out during the 14th century. Its importance is not questioned, however, for it was

here that Dom Fernando I of Portugal and Don Henrique II of Castile signed the Peace of Alcoutim in 1371, bringing peace between their two countries.

The Parish Church, with 16th- and 18th-century features, is perched precariously on the edge of the Guadiana, overlooking its Spanish neighbour, Sanlúcar de Guadiana.

Have a look at the Capela de Misericórdia in the higher central area of the town. A plaque shows the point to which floodwater rose on the disastrous night of 7 December 1876, when the Guadiana rose to unprecedented levels.

It is interesting to take a short trip over the river with the local boatman, or, even better, to go upriver as far as Pomarão.

Looking across the River Guadiana towards Alcoutim from Sanlúcar de Guadiana on the Spanish side. On the left are the castle walls, with the small quay in front of the church on the right and some wooded areas in the background.

Landscape and Crops

This *freguesia* consists of a barren, almost treeless plateau rising to a maximum altitude of 250m. The Ribeira do Vascão which forms the northern boundary, the Ribeira da Foupana in the south and the Ribeira de Cadavais all empty into the Rio Guadiana, and cut deeply into the hard slate and schist. The river valleys are fertile, but are liable to flooding during the occasional heavy rains, with the result that intensive cultivation is limited to areas around small villages, where fruit (mainly oranges) and vegetables are grown.

Fauna, Flora and Birdlife

Bamboo and Oleander grow along the Guadiana, the latter providing a perfect habitat for Nightingales, which seem to sing from every bush in spring. Just back from the river edge, olive, fig, almond and Carob Bean trees are grown where the soil is deep enough, and are often full of Azure-winged Magpies and, in spring, Golden Orioles. White Storks occasionally nest in these trees, but more often on chimneys and church towers (as can be seen in Alcoutim). The hillsides are covered with Gum and Narrow-leaved Cistus, with a few fields of cereals. Eucalyptus is often grown along the roadsides and in a few places com-mercial plantations have been established for wood pulp. Many pure-bred Algarve goats graze these hills – usually distinctly mottled with brown and black on a white background.

Mammals include Red Foxes, which are smaller and darker than their North European counterpart, as well as Wild Boar, Genet, European Mongoose, and Otters by the riversides. The Beech Marten is now becoming rare.

Snakes, especially the Montpellier, are common, but are not dangerous. Huge specimens of the Ocellated Lizard are found within the area.

Butterflies are numerous in the spring and summer near the rivers, including the Scarce Swallowtail, Clouded Yellow, Spanish Marbled White, Blue-spot and Green Hairstreaks, and the Holly and Common Blues.

The Paper-white Narcissus is conspicuous throughout the region during winter and early spring. In damp meadows and river edges large areas are white with the blossom while the air can be heavy with scent. It often flowers at Christmas time.

Chair-making with pine wood is still carried on by some of the older generation. Here, at the time of one of the annual craft exhibitions, one man was showing how he made the woven seats using Bulrush 'tabua'. These chairs are typical of the ones used in many local cottages.

market have one. Smaller, finer baskets with lids are used for needlework.

With all the traditional folk dancing throughout the country, typical white knitted stockings are in demand. Using five needles, working with fine cotton and following long-established patterns, Arminda Cavaco Dionísio in the tiny hamlet of Monte Vascão in the northern Algarve, specializes in these exacting designs, as well as making beautiful Arraiolos carpets. In the same village, Palmira Chaveca makes beautiful crocheted woollen shawls.

Crafts and Local Produce

This river *freguesia* has many associated crafts, including cane or willow basket making in Balurcos and Corte da Seda in particular.

Eurico and Francisco from Balurcos prefer willow to cane, making heavy baskets in two parts – the base and the sides. Using stout uprights, they soak the weaving wands before use. After the circular base has been woven and finished, the uprights are threaded in and the sides are woven, ending with a 'rolled' top. Baskets for vegetables are made with two handles whereas those for

17 SÃO BARTOLOMEU DE MESSINES

The large *freguesia* of São Bartolomeu de Messines is bordered by São Marcos da Serra (10) and São Barnabé (11) to the north, Alte (18) to the east, Silves (35) to the west and Albufeira (40) in the south. It is well situated on the Silves to Barranco do Velho EN124 and the EN264 E01 Seville, Albufeira to Lisbon crossroads. As the town lies within the Silves *concelho*, the parish's Patron Saint is São Bartolomeu.

This typical Algarve chimney is well over 200 years old. These chimneys are very decorative and individual, looking as if they have been fashioned with a fret-saw! In the town are many ancient houses built in the 18th and 19th centuries with wrought iron balconies.

Archaeology and Architecture

This is an old town with many houses in the narrow streets of the centre dating from the 17th century and still retaining their hewn stone lintels. The name 'Messines' suggests that its origins may be connected with Messina in Italy, which is also true of several other villages in the vicinity with similar names.

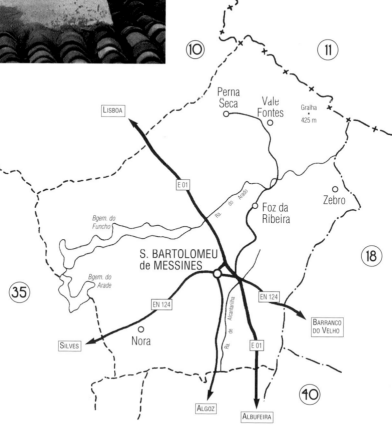

The Parish Church, which is in the centre of the town and partly made of the local red sandstone, dates from the 16th century. It was extensively altered during the 18th century, as is verified by the baroque doorway dated 1716.

Inside, there are three naves with columns in the form of twisted ropes, reminiscent of the Manueline period. Several chapels have 16th-century Manueline vaults or decorative 17th-century glazed tiles. The beautifully carved pulpit is of coloured local marble.

The town is well known for its connections with the 19th-century poet of the Algarve, João de Deus, one of the greatest Portuguese lyric poets of all times. Many streets throughout the area are named after him and his statue graces the town exit on the Silves road.

Landscape and Crops

Geographically, this *freguesia* is diverse. Its highest point is in the north, where the Carboniferous slate rises to 425m at Gralha, near the Algarve–Baixo Alentejo boundary.

The town of São Bartolomeu de Messines is built on Triassic sandstone, which forms a fairly narrow strip running through most of the Algarve parallel to the coast, dividing the limestone of the south from the hard slate of the north. This is relatively hard and dark red in colour, and has been used in the past as a building material for structures such as the Parish Church, the castle at Silves (35), and the portal of the church at Odiáxere (37). It was also used for grinding stones.

The Ribeira de Arade rises high in the Serra de Caldeirão and passes just north of São Bartolomeu de Messines. It has been dammed to create the Barragem do Funcho, before passing on to the Barragem de Arade. The water is used for domestic purposes and for irrigation for fruit (mainly oranges) and vegetables.

The fertile limestone area known as the *barrocal*, lying to the south of São Bartolomeu is planted with many well-managed, mainly small orchards of orange, fig, almond, apricot and peach, plus many vegetable plots.

Fauna, Flora and Birdlife

Mallard and Teal feed on the Funcho reservoir during winter. Come summer the Teal migrates to Northern Europe, leaving the Mallard to breed in the area. Osprey can also be seen here occasionally, feeding on the fish during the winter.

During the autumn and spring migration a large number of birds use the São Marcos Depression, which extends into this *freguesia*, to avoid the higher hills on either side. Melodious Warbler, Nightingale, Pied Flycatcher, Black-eared Wheatear, Wheatear and Rock Thrush all pass through. Storks and vultures often use this route.

Red Foxes and Rabbits are frequently seen, Badgers have their sets in the hills, and Genets are comparatively common, with many seen at night near the Barragem de Arade, crossing the road.

Many species of butterfly can be seen in spring, the commonest being Small Copper, Holly Blue, Spanish Gatekeeper, Clouded Yellow and Spanish Marbled White.

The Spiny-footed Lizard, Moorish Gecko and Iberian Wall Lizard can be seen

Opposite above Almond cakes are a speciality throughout the Algarve, especially in the western region. For special occasions magnificent scenes are made, all in delicious marzipan with delicate colouring. The more mountainous regions are also famous for their honey cakes.

Opposite below The Montpellier Snake is the largest snake in Europe, often measuring over 220cm. This formidable-looking reptile is slightly venomous but the fangs are placed so far back that they are unlikely to harm anyone.

sunning themselves on walls or warm pathways, but are extremely agile if approached. The massive Ocellated Lizard is more often seen in the spring and can give a nasty bite if cornered. Snakes, although common, are mostly seen crossing roads. Only the vary rare Lataste's Viper is venomous. More frequently seen is the very long Montpellier Snake, the adult of which grows to over 2m in length.

Crafts and Local Produce

This is another important honey-producing area, with enormous tracts of unbroken scrubland. In the north-eastern part, *medronho* is made at Zebro, Vale Fontes, Foz de Ribeiro and Perna Seca, as it is at Monte da Zorra in the south of the *freguesia*. Regional marzipan and fig confections with delicious honey cakes (*Bolo de mel*) are also created.

Many local women work at home on crochet and knitting. Alzira Jesus Cabrita in the village of Nora makes beautiful cork 'sculptures'.

18 ALTE

Alte lies in the southern Caldeirão region, and is bounded by São Barnabé (11) to the north, Salir (20) and Benafim (19) to the east, the *concelho* of Albufeira (40) to the south, and São Bartolomeu de Messines (17) to the west. The main EN124 road from Silves to Barranco do Velho passes through, with minor roads to Paderne in the south and many of the northern villages.

The village is generally regarded as one of the most beautiful in Portugal. It is tucked away from the normal tourist routes and consists of steep, narrow, winding *calçada* (cobbled) roads and pathways.

Archaeology and Architecture

Historically interesting, its 1829 church has older parts, in particular the Capela de

Nossa Senhora de Lourdes. Also dating from earlier times are a large number of niches, each supporting a Patron Saint and many decorated with very rare 16th-century *azulejos* of heavy relief in blue, gold, white and maroon from Seville. With the baptismal fonts in the Manueline style, the church as a whole is a combination of architectural forms from the past 500 years, including Arabesque and Manueline.

Close by the Fontes Grande and Pequena a restful, leafy, paved square is interestingly adorned with blue and white *azulejos* depicting the writings of the 20th-

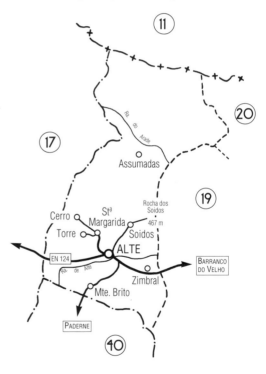

Opposite The magnificent doorway of the Parish Church, which is perched in the middle of this pretty village on the edge of the Caldeirão mountain range. With its steep, quaint, cobbled streets, the village, although becoming a tourist attraction, has retained its original beauty.

century poet Candido Guerreiro. Nearby, Avenida Dr Manuel Teixeira Gomes is named after the noted Algarvean prose writer and statesman who became President of the Republic in 1924, having been the Portuguese Ambassador in London in 1911. (He was the grandfather of the present British Consul in Portimão.)

In nearby Assumadas, Casa Rosa, a small adobe house, has been converted into a mini-museum depicting a typical home of the 19th century with all the utensils needed for living off the land in this remote area. This is the brainchild of the present owners, whose ancestors owned the house, going back to the original Rosa, one of their great-grandparents, many of whose belongings are on show.

One room holds everything necessary for making bread, as well as baskets, bowls and the small hand-operated millstone (*mó*) for grinding wheat. In another room there is period furniture and a cupboard with crockery of the era. This interesting family museum is open to the public from June to the end of September and at other times by appointment

Landscape and Crops
This is another *freguesia* that has a diverse habitat. In the north the land is Carboniferous slate with typical smooth-topped hills and deep cistus-covered valleys. The 467m high, limestone Rocha dos Soidos with its steep escarpments lies near the village of Alte.

The Friar's Cowl is common in all regions. Often known as 'Jack in the Pulpit' it flowers during winter, attractively striped in chocolate and white. In occasional areas a few plants are missing the red gene, thus giving a beautiful golden-coloured flower.

By and large the hillsides are too steep and the soil too thin for cultivation, but where the limestone has been cleared, valuable rich red soil has been planted with oranges and, just south of Alte village, a large vineyard has been established.

In the more sheltered valleys, deep soil washed down by the streams is used for intensive vegetable cultivation, with fruit trees dividing the properties. To the north of Alte in the slate and shale hills, Eucalyptus and pines produce an economic income for an otherwise impoverished region. Carob Bean Trees, some centuries old, provide food for livestock, with any excess sold to a wholesaler in Benafim (19).

Fauna, Flora and Birdlife

The vegetation in the limestone differs greatly from that in the slightly acid Carboniferous slate. Here one finds a multitude of orchids during the springtime, mainly the *Ophrys* group also known as 'Insect Orchids', but also magnificent specimens of the Man Orchid and Naked Man Orchid. During winter, large areas of Paper-white Narcissus grow, especially in moist areas under Almond Trees. By July most of the wild flowers are past, but varieties of Thyme can still be seen in flower on the hillsides, usually with the Curry Plant.

Caves in the limestone cliffs of Rocha dos Soidos are the roosting places for bats, mainly Schreiber's Bat, with colonies of up to a thousand. Surprisingly, though, up to forty of the very rare Mehely's Horseshoe Bat have been found deeper within the same caves.

Crafts and Local Produce

This is an extremely industrious *freguesia* with a large number of diligent artisans living here.

Roughly 5km from Alte on the Santa Margarida road, signposts point the way to where six local women work the lathes, saws and other woodwork equipment to produce the wooden toys at *Da Torre*, their locally well-known workshop in a one-time primary school. Made of pine from northern Portugal, the toys are sanded until very smooth and, with safety in mind, all dowels are made of wood, while non-toxic glue replaces nails and metal screws. The toys are finished with pure wax polish, which is also harmless.

More than 55 models are available, all designed locally, ranging from ferris wheels and carousels to farmyards, dolls' furniture, mobiles and even rocking horses. Dumper trucks, trains, aeroplanes, lorries, caterpillars, grasshoppers, elephants, dogs and ducks are also represented, while different woods with particularly striking grains are used for delightful necklaces, wooden brooches and hair adornments, and attractive paper and pen holders. For these, a clear varnish is usually used rather than the wax.

Back in the hills at Cerro (sometimes written as Serro), the seven ladies of *Confecções de Alte* make all kinds of ladies' clothes, including blouses, skirts and dresses from linen, *broderie anglaise* and natural cotton. Embroidery is often done by machine, although some of the smaller designs are by hand, and the clothing is either ready-made or to measure.

At the *Cerâmica de Alte* on the main EN124, beautiful *azulejos* murals are painted and glazed on the premises. Street and church scenes of Alte are a speciality, but house numbers and even chess boards are also available.

As in other *freguesias* in the region, baskets and mats made from False Esparto Grass are also a speciality.

Amendoinha on the main EN124 through Alte village makes traditional cakes using almonds, nuts, figs, honey, marzipan and many other ingredients. These are also made in nearby Santa Margarida at the *Doçaria Regional Verde Vale (VV)*.

These model paddle boats are just some of the many wooden toys which are made at Torre. Recently some new lines have become very popular, including necklaces using various local woods for the beads, which are strung on leather thongs, and beautifully carved hair clips.

Near to the Benafim boundary in Zimbral, Anabela Guerreiro produces beautiful embroidery using linen as a base, including cushions, place mats, tray cloths, cot sheets, handkerchiefs and lovely dress collars. Initially she machine stitches the material edges and makes a crochet border, before embroidering delicate designs on the linen. Finally she picks up stitches from the crochet edge using two or five very thin needles to knit a border which looks just like fine crochet.

19 BENAFIM

The small *freguesia* of Benafim is bounded by Salir (20) and Querença (25) to the east, the *concelhos* of Loulé (41) and Albufeira (40) to the south, and Alte (18) to the west. Scenically beautiful, it is so far from general tourist routes as to be almost unknown. It is bisected by the EN124 Silves to Barranco do Velho main road, and can also be reached by the minor EN270 road from Boliqueime to Loulé. To the north minor roads lead to Rocha da Pena and Serra do Caldeirão.

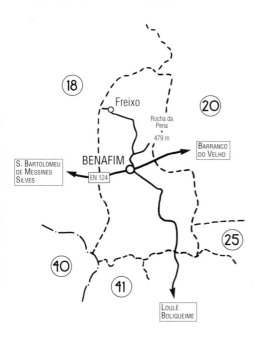

Archaeology and Architecture
Just off the main road within the village, several attractive narrow streets paved with large hewn slabs are lined by pretty little houses, many with typical chimneys, colourful flowers in the tiny gardens and climbers around the doorways, and an array of pot plants.

At nearby Penina a doorway and a chimney date from 1821.

Landscape and Crops
This recently formed *freguesia*, on the north-eastern edge of the *barrocal*, is overlooked by the huge limestone outcrop of Rocha da Pena (Rock of Pity; 479m). Most of the area is scrubland, composed of various cistus species, as well as Strawberry Tree, *Daphne gnidium* and Jerusalem Sage, with a scattering of almond, fig, olive and Carob Bean Trees also forming part of the rural scenery. Small flocks of up to 60 long-legged Churro sheep are grazed on this scrub.

Where the limestone has been laboriously cleared, various fruit trees have been planted, but in the low-lying valley of Freixo more intensive agriculture is practised with large areas of maize, vegetables and fruit. In addition, a large part of the Quinta do Freixo has been designated a *Zona de Caça Turística*, with facilities for game shooting as well as a sophisticated modern clay pigeon range. This 1,176ha estate breeds Pheasants and Red-legged Partridges for strictly controlled shooting. Rabbits, Brown Hares, Turtle Doves, pigeon, Quail and duck are also shot.

Fauna, Flora and Birdlife
The northern part of the *freguesia* is shale and schist, with large areas of Maritime Pine and Eucalyptus, through which flocks of noisy, gregarious Azure-winged Magpies fly. Great and Blue Tits and the occasional family of Long-tailed Tits inhabit the pine woods. Red-legged Partridge coveys are seen, especially during spring, the female quietly gathering her brood together to lead them to safety. Short-toed Eagles with pale underparts can often be seen overhead, with their characteristic slow flapping, as they hover looking for snakes and other reptiles which form their main source of food.

The usual mammal life is present, with Red Fox, Rabbit, Brown Hare, Egyptian Mongoose, Genet and Wild Boar mainly in the scrub hillsides.

Butterflies are very common during spring. Small Copper, Lang's Short-tailed Blue and Green Hairstreak are often on the wing in early spring, quickly followed by the Cleopatra and Spanish Festoon. With the heat of summer the quantity of

The great limestone outcrops of Rocha da Pena and Rocha dos Soidos are visible from most areas in this *freguesia*. Surrounded by hard Carboniferous slate covered with cistus scrub, these outcrops are a botanist's paradise, with many species of orchid in particular to be found.

The Common Toad is found in most habitats. The female is considerably larger than the male and often more than 15cm long. The toad is basically nocturnal, hiding under leaves or even stones during the daytime. It has a characteristic red eye with a horizontal pupil.

species diminishes, but there is a marked increase for a short time during autumn.

Crafts and Local Produce

Little in the *artesanato* line goes on in the village, but within the hills, as in so many areas where the Strawberry Tree grows, *medronho* is distilled. This 'firewater' is made mainly in the south of Portugal,

where the slightly acidic soil and optimum climatic conditions encourage the tree's profuse growth and production. The casks in which it is stored are made to the north in Oporto. They were previously made of oak, which is much better than the chestnut primarily used now. The colour of *medronho* depends largely on the type of wood used to mature it, combined with the age of the casks.

The ripe fruit is placed in enormous barrels, then covered with water and some other cover to protect against bacterial infection. The cover varies from a thin layer of sand, to a layer of plastic covered with sand. In some instances, though, it is left open and the top removed as far as the 'sweet' liquid at the time of distillation.

Fermentation takes about two months, during which time a thick, brownish scum

At Zimbral, on the border between Benafim and Alte, delightful linen is beautifully embroidered before its border is knitted using very fine needles. For circular, square or rectangular pieces the knitting is worked with five needles.

looking like a hard lid or crust forms on top of the barrel. The *medronho* cannot be distilled until all fermentation has ceased. Each barrel holds about 40 *arrôbas* (600kg) and makes around 100 litres.

A '*Medronho* Work Team' coordinated by IN LOCO, the University of the Algarve and the Department of Agriculture is trying to improve the whole fermentation process, since without any contact with air it should ideally take a maximum of two weeks.

The fruit and the fermented liquid are placed in enclosed copper stills and heated. Copper tubes coiled through cold water collect the steam, which is cooled rapidly. The resultant spirit then slowly drips into containers.

The sign of a good *medronho* is the number and size of the bubbles which remain on top after it has been shaken.

20 SALIR

This Algarve *freguesia* is bounded by São Barnabé (11) and Ameixial (12) to the north, Cachopo (21) and São Brás de Alportel (26) eastwards, Querença (25) southwards, and Benafim (19) and Alte (18) to the west. It is well situated on the Silves to Barranco do Velho EN124, with a good road to Loulé en route to either Faro EN125-4 or Quarteira EN396. Minor roads lead into the Caldeirão mountains, in particular a small one through Malhão and Sitio das Éguas to São Barnabé and Almodôvar.

Archaeology and Architecture
One or two walls from the old Arabic castle can be seen on the western edge of the village. The church on the eastern side, currently being restored, has some interesting

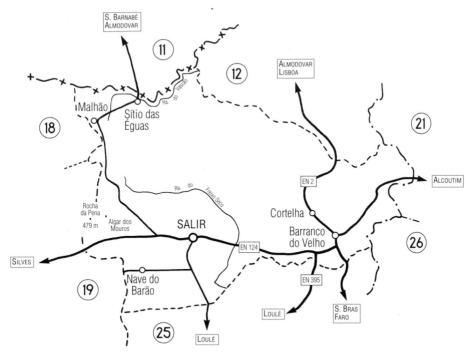

Salir castle is strategically placed, now overlooking the EN124 in the valley below. This old Moorish castle is in ruins with very little remaining, but it still offers fabulous views over the village to the church. To the west is the impressive Rocha da Pena.

azulejos. New wooden floors are being installed and the gold leaf is being renewed in Moncarapacho. The church was originally a mosque with three naves and plain columns, but was extensively damaged by the 1755 earthquake. Of the original, only the altar area remains.

From the top of Rocha da Pena (Rock of Pity), two 800m long walls are believed to date from the Neolithic Age. Nearby at Algar dos Mouros (Cave of the Moors), there are Arabic remains dating from the 13th century, when it is said that the Moors took refuge here from Salir at the time of the Christian reconquest of the Algarve.

Landscape and Crops
From all parts of the *freguesia*, the huge limestone mountain of Rocha da Pena can be seen, distinctively flat topped and surrounded by steep escarpments. In 1993 it was declared a 'classified site' due to its unique flora and fauna, and the fact that it is an almost isolated limestone intrusion in the Carboniferous slate zone.

In valleys near Salir fruit and vegetables are intensively cultivated in the deep red soil produced from decomposed limestone rock. Nearby vineyards produce rosé wine. Carob Bean and Almond Trees are grown extensively and, in the higher land, cork is harvested. Eucalyptus and Maritime Pine are interspersed throughout.

Fauna, Flora and Birdlife
The plant life on the limestone (*barrocal*) is rich and various. *Allium pruinatum* and *Bellevalia hackelii* are endemic throughout the Algarve and can be found within the maquis and garigue scrub on the hillsides, along with many species of *Orchis* and *Ophrys*. Narcissi, especially the Hoop Petticoat, are abundant in early spring, carpeting the ground together with the Barbary Nut (*Iris sisyrinchium*). The native cistus species are the dominant shrubs, with

Right The Yellow Bee Orchid with the common *Fedia cornucopia* growing together in moist grassland during early April. *Fedia* is one of the early flowering plants and can usually be seen from January onwards. Note the drops of dew on the orchid flower!

Cistus populifolius in the slate and shale areas. Occasionally these plants are parasitized by the strange but beautiful *Cytinus ruber*, the red and yellow flowers of which push through the soil. *Paeonia broteroi* usually adds colour to the hillsides in April.

The Rocha da Pena is a well-known area for the huge Eagle Owl, which, along with Bonelli's Eagle and Buzzard, is said to nest on the escarpment.

During summer, Bee-eaters twist and dive after insects. Alpine Swifts, the largest of the swifts with white underparts, fly at higher altitudes, and many warblers nest in the cistus scrub.

The Algar dos Mouros cave in the limestone cliffs is home to a large population of Schreiber's Bat and a few Lesser Mouse-eared bats.

Red Fox, Genet and Egyptian Mongoose are common, and Hedgehogs are frequently found in the cultivated land near the villages.

Crafts and Local Produce
The shop in Salir co-funded by the EC programme LEADER, the IN LOCO managed project for the Caldeirão mountains, is known as *Casa da Serra*. It is full of products from the many small workshops, societies, co-operatives and individual contributors throughout the area: wooden toys from Torre near Alte, *medronho* and honey from Almodôvar, delicious biscuits from Alte and rosé wine from Nave do Barão in the Salir *freguesia*, baskets made from False Esparto grass or palm (made at the shop by the two ladies who are responsible for the day to day sales; see below), rag dolls from Ameixial

and jute dolls from Martinlongo, beautiful jumpers from Cachopo, weaving from *A Lançadeira* also in Cachopo, miniature *albardas* and *molins* (donkey saddles and mule collars), blouses from Alte and beautifully embroidered linen from Zimbral, woven wares from Almodôvar made from T-shirt offcuts, ceramic plates and cork models from Santana da Serra and organically grown herbs from Martinlongo. A collection of postcards showing scenes within the mountains are produced by IN LOCO and are available at the shop.

Empreita baskets are made from wild Dwarf Palm leaves, which are picked and dried when green. After being moistened, they are cut into equal widths and made into wide plaits, which are machined together to make baskets, place mats or bags. Alternatively, some baskets are made by conventional weaving. Medium-sized, machined baskets require eight *braças* (double arm's width) of plaited palm!

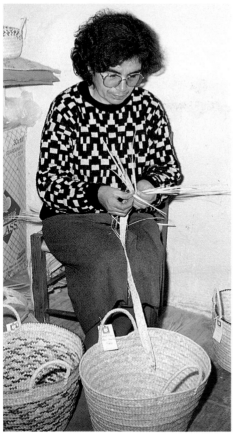

In the *Casa da Serra* craft shop in Salir you can always find either Dwarf Fan Palm or False Esparto baskets being made by one of the ladies who manage the shop. They have plenty of examples of their work and that of other artisans for sale.

The handles are made of the same material by twisting two palm lengths, each of which is given a treble twist before being entwined together, and then repeating the process. This makes a cord, with three or four lengths joined together to form a handle which is bound with the same material. Two *braças* make a handle!

Esparto baskets, as the name suggests, are made from False Esparto. The method is similar to *empreita* work, but all *esparto* work is stitched by hand.

21 CACHOPO

Cachopo is bounded by Ameixial (12) and Salir (20) to the west, Martinlongo (13) to the north, Vaqueiros (22) to the east, and São Brás de Alportel (26), Santa Catarina da Fonte do Bispo (27), and Tavira (44) to the south. It is strategically placed on both the EN124, Barranco do Velho to Alcoutim road and the EN397 from Tavira on the southern coast, as well as on a minor road from Furnazinhas in the east and a hard-core track from Ameixial in the west.

Archaeology and Architecture
The church of Santo Estêvão is set within the village and is well known for its pilgrimages.

The dolmen of Pedras Altas can be seen at Mealha, and Celtic round houses, now used as grain stores, can also be found in the same area. An unusual feature of this region are the strange thatched straw and hay stacks.

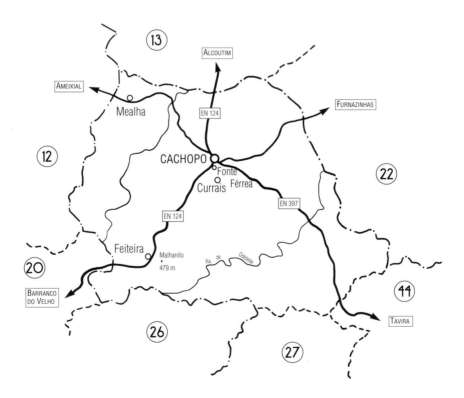

Cork Oaks are stripped from the end of July onwards. Sap from the remaining live bark (only dead bark is removed) turns russet in the sunlight, darkening later. Cork is stripped every nine years (the lower part of this tree was cut a few years earlier), and numbers on the trunk refer to the last year of stripping.

Landscape and Crops

This is a large *freguesia* with a bedrock very similar to the slate and shale of its neighbouring areas. It offers spectacular scenery with deep ravines and high round-topped hills, but has a much higher rainfall than the coastline, sometimes reaching 1,000mm per year. This provides sufficient moisture to sustain thick vegetation in the valleys.

The main income is derived from cork which, when cut, is neatly stacked for a year to cure and dry before being sent to factories for processing. It is notable that the younger population has declined in numbers to the extent that in Feiteira the local football ground is now used for stacking and drying cork. Near this village is the highest point in the *freguesia*, at 541m.

Fauna, Flora and Birdlife

Within the cork woods birds are numerous and include Green, Great Spotted and Lesser Spotted Woodpeckers. The latter is hardly larger than a sparrow and is difficult to locate due to its camouflage colouring. Short-toed Treecreepers and Nuthatches can be seen foraging up and down the fissured bark of the trees for insects, and Woodlarks sing from prominent vantage points. Great, Blue, Long-tailed and, surprisingly, Crested Tits swing from the branches of the Cork Oak (the Crested Tit is more frequently found in coniferous woods).

If you walk up the valley of Fonte Férrea on the EN124 from Barranco do Velho on the outskirts of Cachopo, you may see Chaffinch, Wren, Dartford and Sardinian

The strange parasitic *Cytinus ruber* attaches itself to the roots of cistus species, gaining all its nourishment from the host plant. It is found throughout the area and flowers during the late spring.

Warbler, as well as many other woodland birds. During the summer Rock Buntings are frequently spotted, along with the Melodious Warbler and the Nightingale.

Many small butterflies flutter through the undergrowth. Grizzled, Mallow, Lulworth and Essex Skippers are relatively common, but there are many geographical variations within this group which make identification difficult. Blues are common, as are Cleopatra, Swallowtail, Spanish Marbled White and, where the Strawberry Tree grows, the Two-tailed Pasha.

Dragonflies patrol water courses, especially the Ruddy Darter and in long stretches of water the Emperor Dragonfly, although these also stray into cool woodland. As many dragonflies are migrants, unusual African species are sometimes found, such as *Brachythemis leucosticta* in autumn.

During spring the roadsides are lined with the yellow-flowered Broom, planted many years ago by the road builders (*cantoneiros*). Underneath the Cork Trees, Lavender, Tree Heather and cistus create a colourful scene.

Crafts and Local Produce

Pig breeding and the subsequent production of *chouriça* and *presunto* is very important to the local economy.

This is an industrious village, with specialist blacksmiths and two mule-collar and donkey-saddle makers.

A Lançadeira (The Shuttle) is run by four ladies and has a total of eight looms of varying sizes, from large ones for heavy curtain materials (of which up to 3m can be woven daily) to small ones for delicate scarves, table mats and runners. Raised patterns are made every fourth or fifth stitch by the weft being looped over a wire, followed by another weft thread. The wire is then removed leaving a pretty raised effect. Equally, intricate tapestries are slowly and painstakingly worked.

This shows a large loom in use. It takes two days to set up one of the larger looms which can weave a maximum width of 230cm and up to 30m in length. On the more simple designs up to 3m can be worked daily.

Natural colours are most common, but some vegetable dyes are also used: Gum Cistus for pale greenish-yellow and French Lavender for very pale blue. A number of products are made from linen or cotton, from curtain materials to tote bags. The designs are worked out on the premises using mainly browns and fawns from natural dyes.

Wool is also used to effect, much of it received in its original state and carded here. It is then spun on an extremely old spinning wheel, before another home-made wheel is used for loading the shuttles. Some of the softest scarves are in white wool and have delicate texture effects in the traditional diamond *montanhac* design, which is achieved from the layout of the warp.

Another group of women at *Malhas de Cachopo* produce machine-knitted jumpers, which are individually finished with delightful hand-embroidered designs of local flowers.

In the small hamlet of Currais, Maria Rosário specializes in dried flowers of the area. Traditional woollen blankets, Arraiolos rugs and crochet work are made to order.

22 VAQUEIROS

Vaqueiros is bounded by Martinlongo (13), Giões (14) and Pereiro (15) to the north, Odeleite (23) to the east, Tavira (44) to the south and Cachopo (21) westwards. It is accessible from Martinlongo by the 506 minor road, or from Cachopo by the 505.

Archaeology and Architecture
This small village was built on an Arab settlement and has an attractive church which was completely restored in the 18th century. White storks now nest on top.

Landscape and Crops
This is a remote and wild *freguesia* with many villages lost in a bygone age and suffering from a declining population. The area is crossed by the Ribeira da Foupana, with its tributary the Ribeira da Foupanilha in the north and the Ribeira de Odeleite in the centre cutting through the hard slate bedrock. A high plateau (333m) is rifted by deep valleys, richly vegetated with reeds, Oleander and Aspen lining the banks. Small areas of grain are grown where there is sufficient depth of soil on the hillsides. The sparse grassland and cistus scrub is grazed by sheep and goats.

The river valleys where most of the villages are situated are fertile and produce fruit and vegetables to sustain the local population. In many areas the cistus is cut in rotation to

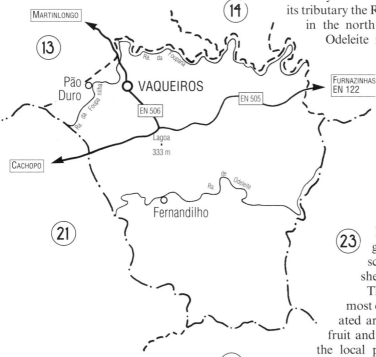

provide fuel for baking. Many of the large estates in the area are being converted into reserved hunting areas, into which native game is being introduced and managed, thus providing another source of income.

A typical shepherd's hut perched high on a hillside overlooking the Ribeira da Foupanilha, near the small village of Pão Duro. These are usually made simply from the scrub and covered with straw or reeds. They are both waterproof and windproof.

Fauna, Flora and Birdlife
Within the river valleys Narcissi grow in quantity. The Paper-white is the first to flower around Christmas time, followed in early spring by the beautiful Hoop Petti-coat which is found in more stony locations. During spring many small rivers support quantities of highly scented *Narcissus jonquilla* (Jonquils), which are also

planted in cottage gardens. In the degenerated garigue which has been grazed by goats and sheep, there is a riot of colour for a short period during spring as many bulbous and annual plants emerge from the dry ground after the first rains. Iris and asphodel with its attractive spike of white flowers cover large areas, along with the tall yellow *Linaria*, the minute purple *Linaria amethystea* and the annual *Helianthemum* with yellow petals and a brown centre. Odd patches of the red-flowered dock are more commonly seen on the Alentejo plains.

During winter large flocks of Golden Plovers feed on the land, while large numbers of migrating birds, especially Wheatears and Yellow Wagtail, can be seen crossing the hillsides. The river valleys are full of the smaller passerines, including Stonechat, Crested Lark, Grey Wagtail, Black Redstart, Goldfinch and Serin, plus a host of warblers.

Mammal numbers are not as great as in the more populated areas, but Wild Boar are found in the river valleys with Red Fox, Egyptian Mongoose, Rabbit, Brown Hare and Genet. Red Deer introduced for sporting purposes are sometimes seen in the vicinity of hunting reserves.

Crafts and Local Produce
Within the village both José Manuel Pedro and Henrique Martins make miniature wooden models from Oleander or Alder woods. Cows and carts, chairs, rocking horses and many more interesting items are made by these gifted artisans.

The tiny hamlet of Pão Duro high above the Ribeira da Foupanilha is set amidst the most beautiful scenery, completely away from the tourist routes. Here, Dona Florinda makes *Licor de Poejo* (Pennyroyal liqueur). The Pennyroyal is either collected in the spring from the river valleys, or, as in this case, sown in special locations and picked at a much later date. After picking it is dried for a week in the sun.

To make the liqueur, a teacupful of the dried herbs is cut finely with scissors and left for about ten days steeping in *aguardente de medronho*. Next, 1kg of sugar is dissolved in about three quarters of a litre of boiling water to produce a syrup. After straining the herb from the spirit mixture, the remaining fortified liquid is added to the syrup and bottled. After about three months it is ready for drinking. According to Dona Florinda, it is a good remedy for 'flu, especially if local honey is added'.

Another local craft specialist is Maria Claudina da Silva Marta from the tiny hamlet of Fernandilho. She makes small baskets and lightweight containers from *palhinhas*, the dried stems of a very fine grass. The grass is dampened and then, in mini-bundles, wound in spirals, before being stitched approximately every half centimetre to hold it in place.

Opposite These delightful small baskets and mats from the small hamlet of Fernandilho are made from the stems of a very fine dried grass. The dampened bundles of grass are wound round and stitched into place. This is very time consuming and complicated work.

On a musical note, the 'Song of the Souls' (*canção das almas*) which is sung throughout the Algarve comes from the small hamlet of Cabaços in the south of the *freguesia*.

23 ODELEITE AND 24 AZINHAL

The natural history and geology of Odeleite and Azinhal are very similar.

Landscape and Crops
The Guadiana River, fed by the Ribeira de Odeleite and Ribeira de Beliche, cuts through hard slate to form the eastern

A quiet bank on the edge of the Rio Guadiana. These typical river boats are used by the local fishermen to catch eels, Grey Mullet and Lampreys. Spain is on the far bank as the river here divides the two countries.

boundary. Just south of Odeleite, a huge reservoir is being constructed which, together with the Barragem de Beliche, will eventually provide irrigation and domestic water for the south-eastern region of the Algarve.

Away from the river banks, the thin soil sustains pasture and cistus scrub, which in turn feed a large population of goats, most of them belonging to the pedigree Raça Algarvia and are registered in the herd book of ANCCRAL, whose offices are in Azinhal.

Cereals are grown on the hillsides, and vegetables, maize and fruit in the fertile river valleys, including orange groves where adequate irrigation is available. Almonds and Carob Bean Trees are an important source of income and can be grown on the poorer, drier land.

Fauna, Flora and Birdlife

The Guadiana is tidal in the *freguesia* and brings Lesser Black-backed and Black-headed Gulls, while Little Terns can be seen diving after Sand Eels and small fish. The 'inland' terns pass on migration and many Black Terns are seen during spring and autumn. One of the specialities of the region is the Rufus Bushchat, which can often be sighted perched on a tree or telephone wire.

Reeds, Bamboo and Osier flourish along the rivers, providing material for basket weaving, for which the area –

The extraordinary Black-winged Stilt is basically a summer visitor to ponds, lakes and salt marshes where there is shallow water. It nests in tufts of reeds or amongst lakeside vegetation, and has the longest legs in proportion to its body of any bird.

especially around Odeleite – is renowned. Similarly, Oleander grows in the streams near Azinhal, its hard, lightweight wood being carved for bobbins for lace making.

Early in the year the Cleopatra butterfly can be seen near the river, but is often confused with the Brimstone, which is also present. The distinguishing feature is the orange mark on the forewing of the Cleopatra. Over-wintering Red Admiral are often seen during the spring, and April brings forth a multitude of butterflies looking for food plants on which to lay their eggs.

Otters are found in the rivers, and the rare Beech Marten can be seen. An extremely large form of the Ocellated Lizard usually found further north is occasionally spotted near the river.

23 ODELEITE

Odeleite *freguesia* is bordered by the Rio Guadiana to the east, Azinhal (24) and Tavira (44) to the south, Vaqueiros (22) to the west, and Pereiro (15) and Alcoutim (16) to the north. The Vila Real de Santo António to Mértola EN122 passes through the area, and several smaller roads skirt the river.

This is a delightful area with the village of Odeleite perched on a hilltop in the surrounding hills, overlooking the River Odeleite (roughly translated as river of milk). Built on the hilly slopes, all the houses bordering the narrow streets seem to be on different levels.

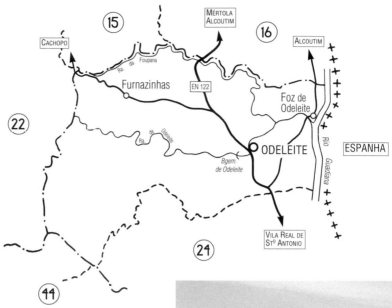

Archaeology and Architecture

The interesting, but comparatively plain Parish Church with its three naves dominates the small village, but unlike many others is set low down in the valley.

Here enormous canes are often stripped of their leafy outer skin and used for roofing, *caniço de casa*, the typical 'under the tile lining' which is so attractive.

Crafts and Local Produce

António Domingos Sequeira Gonçalves, once a member of the Portuguese Marines, is a specialist basket maker in this parish. His claim to fame is not only basketry, however, for he is also known locally for his strength as a swimmer. His early training was just for fun up and down the beautiful Odeleite, but in 1956 he won the 100 yards breast stroke at the Sail Training Ships regatta in Dartmouth, England, when he was a crew member of the *Sagres* tall-ship training ship, and then in August 1991, at the age of 55, he swam down the Guadiana

A cane-basket maker standing by a wall opposite his home, which overlooks the Ribeira de Odeleite. The canes are collected from the banks of the river. The largest basket is for bread, which is made weekly in several outlying villages. It keeps the bread fresh and vermin-proof.

River from Foz de Odeleite to Vila Real de Santo António, a distance of approximately 18km, in four hours and one minute.

He makes large covered bread containers, *canastra condensa*, which look like linen baskets. These are still used in the Alentejo where home-baked bread is made weekly and must be kept clean, vermin-proof and permeated with fresh air.

Intriguing basket-work 'tubes' called *canastros*, just over 1m high with a diameter of 35cm, often stand by the roadside. In less populated areas of the Algarve these are used as protection for young Cork, Carob Bean, Strawberry Tree, citrus and other fruit trees against 'bark-eaters' such as domestic goats and sheep, Rabbits and Wild Boar.

After preparing the canes by stripping the outer leafy coat with a sickle, one man can make about three *canastros* per hour. A deep container is filled with wet soil, and seven holes are made around the outside before drying until solid to produce the working form. Canes are inserted in the holes, each just over 1m in length, after which they are woven with split canes until the required height is reached.

Honey and cheese are produced in the village of Furnazinhas, with honey cakes and confections made to order.

minor roads eastwards to the river or westwards to the Barragem de Beliche and the interior beyond.

This delightful village within the concelho of Castro Marim is one of six Algarve Azinhals, a name which is literally translated as 'grove of Holm Oaks'. Although it is on the main eastern route of the Algarve it retains the feeling of a bygone age.

Archaeology and Architecture
The unusual church on the eastern edge of the village has a cupola which gives a lighthouse effect, a rounded nave and a mini spire. Just beyond the church and nearer to the River Guadiana and the Spanish border is a disused windmill, from where there are magnificent views. It's worthwhile coming here to appreciate this special part of southern Portugal.

Crafts and Local Produce
This *freguesia* still practises many original crafts and is particularly famous for its bobbin lace, a cottage craft which has fast declined in recent years. Courses are held for younger people in Vila Real de Santo António, and Silves is the only council which trains children from the age of six.

24 AZINHAL

Azinhal is skirted by the Rio Guadiana to the east and bounded by Castro Marim/Vila Real de Santo António (45) to the south, Tavira (44) to the southwest, and Odeleite (23) to the north. Its main access is via the EN122 Vila Real de Santo António to Mértola road, with

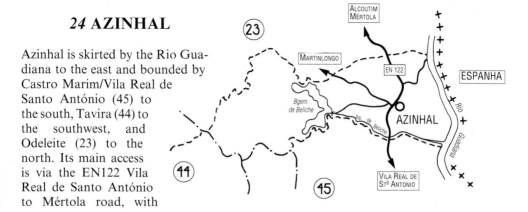

Lizards are usually rather nervous creatures and vanish from sight at the first sign of danger. They are often seen sunning themselves on rocks, walls or pathways, but are less common in southern Portugal than further east in Europe. The most common variety is the Iberian Wall Lizard.

The origin of pillow or bobbin lace is lost in the mists of time. Belgium, Spain and France first produced this beautiful work at almost the same time, with the original 'lace' made of the finest straw. Some of the older women in Azinhal learnt this craft at school, and many work with white thread, on white patterns, on white cushions, which gives enormous eye strain (normally patterns are on coloured paper or parchment).

Left This gnarled olive tree serves as a garage for the mule cart and gives all-year protection (olive trees are not deciduous). The fruit, which is picked during early winter, is pickled for bar appetizers or for using in many typical culinary dishes, as well as being pressed for olive oil.

Right Azinhal is the area's home of bobbin lace, and many housewives in the village can be found working on traditional patterns – hard work, since they are white and use white cotton only relieved by coloured pins. The Oleander wood bobbins are carved in the village.

The bobbins are about 18cm long and made from Oleander wood, all beautifully carved. The ladies rapidly click-clack anything from 60 to an incredible 120 bobbins together to make this traditional lace. Pins hold the work together, retaining the tension from one part of the design to another. Lace is in reality a form of weaving, with the spacing according to the twisting of the threads. The closer the weave, the more time it takes, and cost is dependent upon this.

The Portuguese home of bobbin lace is Vila do Conde (north of Oporto), where the museum has many spectacular pieces. One local lady is making a piece to order for the museum using two thousand bobbins!

José Vaz Pereira is the only remaining bobbin maker in Azinhal, producing about four per hour by cutting the Oleander wood into shape with a sharp knife and then sandpapering it until completely smooth.

25 QUERENÇA

Querença is bordered by Loulé (41) to the south, São Brás de Alportel (26) eastwards, Salir (20) to the north and Benafim (19) to the west. It is situated on the EN396 from Quarteira on the coast

The delightful church square showing the Parish Church and antique cross. Many of the Serra do Caldeirão villages have their own special beauty; one visitor to Querença, on seeing us taking photographs, remarked 'You are portraying Paradise!'

through Loulé to Barranco do Velho, with several minor roads branching into the surrounding countryside.

Archaeology and Architecture
This is a small *freguesia* of 2,000 inhabitants with an area of only 60 sq km. Its monuments are noteworthy, however, including a Roman bridge at Tôr and the interesting Manor House in Querença, which now houses the offices of the Parish Council.

Querença's Church of Nossa Senhora da Assunção is situated opposite the Manor House in a large square at an altitude of 276m. Dating from 1745, it is small but impressive, having been extensively restored in 1966. Its origins are much older, though, and are attributed to the Knights Templars of Santiago from AD 1500. Its Manueline doorway (recorded in 1518 in the parish records) bears testimony to this date, for the Manueline period lasted roughly from 1460 to 1520. The beautiful interior depicts grapes and olives, figs and doves, all in spectacular gold leaf.

Within the square near the Manor House is a cross of uncertain date. The actual inscription on the cross has been partly reconstructed and looks like 1653, but according to the record book it could be either 1632 or 1832.

Tôr, a small village with quaint narrow streets, is well worth browsing around. In Pombal, a small hamlet joining Querença, a

traditional *nora* (water wheel) was restored during 1993, while at Fonte Filipe a river mill will shortly be in working order again. Nearby Cerro dos Negros (404m) is the highest point in the *freguesia*.

Fauna, Flora and Birdlife

On 10 October 1991, Fonte da Benémola was declared a classified site to protect its unique flora and fauna plus its outstanding beauty. The rivers cut through both dolomitic limestone and shale, giving differing flora in each locality, with the limestone at Salustreira forming two caves which house Mehely's and Lesser Horseshoe, Lesser Mouse-eared and Schreiber's Bats. It was here in 1978 that the Lesser Mouse-eared Bat was first found in Portugal.

In the river valley vegetables are produced in the deep loam, while the river sides are edged with Giant Reed, which is used for basket making. On the hillsides typical cistus scrub forms the undergrowth for Cork Oaks and pines. Along path edges in grassland areas, orchids are abundant, notably the Man, Woodcock and Yellow Bee Orchids and the Portuguese form of the Mirror Orchid.

On shale slopes Carob Bean and Cork Oaks are predominant, but in some areas the latter have been superseded by the Western Iberian form of the Ilex Oak where the undergrowth is Kermes Oak and Mastic Tree with Gum, Grey-leaved and Narrow-leaved Cistus.

During summer Golden Orioles and Nightingales are common in the valleys and orchards, with Bee-eaters diving after insects overhead. All year round Great Spotted Woodpeckers, Short-toed Treecreepers, Great Tits and occasional Blue and Long-tailed Tits can be seen in the cork woods, and Kingfishers in the river valleys. Warblers, including the Dartford and Sardinian, are always present in the low undergrowth.

Mammals are rarely seen, although family groups of Egyptian Mongoose often cross the hillsides during the day. Otter and the nocturnal Genet, which is mainly arboreal, are almost as common as Rabbit and Red Fox.

The Strawberry Tree is an attractive, slow-growing, small tree with urn-shaped cream flowers and fruit forming simultaneously in the autumn. The globular red fruit is used to distil the potent *medronho*. The hard wood is much prized for wood carving.

In the scrubland butterflies are numerous with many skippers, blues and fritillaries. The Swallowtail and Scarce Swallowtail are commonly seen, and where the Strawberry Tree grows the Two-tailed Pasha is found during May and late summer.

Crafts and Local Produce

The traditional craft of basket weaving from the Giant Reed is carried out along the Benémola river valley. The hand-operated stripping machine is rather primitive, but certainly makes this exacting work much easier.

Some of the older generation continue making *medronho* in the old-fashioned way, but this will soon be replaced by modern methods due to EC regulations.

The making of rag dolls is an art which has come to the fore during the last few years and you will find extremely attractive examples in traditional regional working costume. These dolls stand about 25cm high and are made from strong wire which is 'bandaged' with rags and covered with sorbo and cloth to give the final shape. To finish off, they are fully dressed, complete with miniature shoes. Each doll takes anything from five hours upwards to complete.

Just outside Querença, as with many places throughout areas which have the Strawberry Tree, *medronho* is distilled. This strong spirit warms fishermen after a long chilly night on the sea, or is used for flaming *chouriça* or as an after-dinner liqueur in local restaurants.

Dona Filipa Faísca de Sousa from Borno is a true artist with many strings to her bow. She makes the dolls' accessories – knitted stockings and woven hats, plus bread ovens and millstones out of cement! Her scenes are of cereal winnowing and sacking, the complete bread-making process, or drawing water from the original Moorish-type wells. She was the teacher for a group in the *freguesia* of Ameixial (12) further north in the Algarve, and is also a well known local poet.

In Pombal delicious ice-cream is made using all natural ingredients.

26 SÃO BRÁS DE ALPORTEL

São Brás de Alportel is bordered by Faro (42) and Olhão (43) to the south, Santa Catarina da Fonte do Bispo (27) to the east, Cachopo (21) northwards and Salir (20) and Querença (25) to the west. It is strategically located on the northern EN2 from Faro and the inland EN270 from Quarteira and Loulé to Santa Catarina da Fonte do Bispo and Tavira.

This area is well worth a visit. Often overlooked, it occupies a beautiful setting which justifies its reputation of 'nestling between the mountains and the ocean'.

Archaeology and Architecture

The Parish Church of São Brás de Alportel is situated in an attractive tree-lined square, surrounded by period houses and overlooking fabulous countryside which stretches to the south coast. Inside the church the Capela do Senhor dos Passos is filled with gilded woodwork.

The Museu Etnográfico do Trajo Algarvio is an interesting ethnographic museum located in the older part of the town on the Tavira road. It usually has ongoing exhibitions, but also boasts a fascinating permanent collection of Algarve memorabilia, including ancient presses for processing cork, huge hand-operated machinery for making metal rims for carts, all types of carriages, water carts, wine carts, saddlery and ploughs, plus a forge with enormous bellows. In addition there are many reproduction costumes of bygone days made by *Lançadeira* workshop in Cachopo (21).

Landscape and Crops

The geology of this *freguesia* is complex. The southern part is hard limestone while São Brás de Alportel itself lies on the narrow strip of red sandstone which divides the limestone from the hard slate of the northern area. The highest point is 529m, just south of the village of Javali ('Wild Boar'). To the north of the town, Eucalyptus and Maritime Pines are grown commercially, with many hillsides mechanically terraced to facilitate Eucalyptus plantations. The natural vegetation is Cork Oak with an undergrowth of cistus and

Strawberry Tree. The fertile valleys produce vegetables and fruit, especially near the scattered villages, and the southern part of the *freguesia* is rich with a large number of orchids which flourish throughout the spring, usually starting in February with the Sawfly Orchid and finishing in early June with the Pyramidal Orchid.

Here the Carob Bean Tree comes into its own, with huge trees many decades old laden with long black bean pods from mid-July onwards. Their use varies from stock feed and chocolate substitute to the pharmaceutical industry, and in some areas the pods are ground and mixed with wheat flour to make a delicious heavy black bread. Almonds and figs grow in the fields, interspersed with wheat or oats, and where irrigation is possible, there is intensive vegetable cultivation.

Fauna, Flora and Birdlife

This exceptionally beautiful stretch of countryside is enhanced by a wealth of butterflies and moths. Among the butterflies the Clouded Yellow is common, especially in fields of lucerne and other species of clover. It is a very variable species with many geographical forms throughout Europe. Lang's Short-tailed Blue is possibly the most wide-spread and can be seen throughout the year, as it can produce up to three generations annually. The Striped and Silver-striped Hawk Moths are also numerous, especially in vineyards.

Genets, Egyptian Mongoose and Wild Boar inhabit the scrubland, and Hedgehogs frequent gardens and cultivated land.

All three of southern Portugal's woodpeckers can be found – the Great and Lesser Spotted, and the Green, which is distinctly yellower than its northern European counterpart. It is often seen probing the turf for insects, especially ants, with its long sticky tongue. The Wryneck, which is also a species of Woodpecker, is a passing migrant.

Hoopoes are frequently seen searching for insects on short grass, lawns and, further to the south, golf-courses. Many of the warblers inhabit this area, as well as flocks of Goldfinches feeding on Teasel and thistle seeds.

This small village, situated remotely in the hills, typifies the hard and precarious living experienced by the people of the region. Most of their income is derived from cork and honey production, which has resulted in many of the younger generation seeking more lucrative jobs elsewhere.

Crafts and Local Produce

José Viegas from São Brás de Alportel makes brushes from dried Dwarf Fan Palm leaves. A cord passes through a ring on a board which he then attaches to his belt to retain an even tension. Taking a double division of a large palm leaf he folds the stem end over this tight cord and binds it in place with a fine palm length. This procedure is repeated until the bound pieces are sufficient to surround a dried Bamboo cane. After beating the palm flat with a hammer he binds it onto the cane, ending with the cord end firmly secured within the binding. One nail is used to completely secure the brush head onto the handle. After cutting the 'bristles' level, they can be beaten over a contraption which looks like a 'bed of nails' to give a fine feathery finish.

In Mesquita Baixa just off the road to Tavira, an old olive oil cellar has been reno-

Above The Carob Bean is important commercially. These green immature pods become mahogany coloured when mature, and are used in the pharmaceutical industry, for animal feeds, or locally for delicious bread. Mature seeds are all identical in weight and are still used in Arab countries as weights for gold and silver, hence the 'carat'.

Right Making Dwarf Fan Palm brushes. The final fixing of the prepared brush 'bristles' onto the handle before securing them with a single nail to prevent the head from being removed. The next step is to trim all to the same length with a very sharp knife.

vated with partial funding from the LEADER programme and will soon be opened as a Cultural and Gastronomic Centre to promote the traditions of the *Serra* villages.

This is another *freguesia* where delicious fig and almond confections are made, in both the town itself and also in Juncais.

27 SANTA CATARINA DA FONTE DO BISPO

Santa Catarina da Fonte do Bispo is bordered by São Brás de Alportel (26) to the west, Cachopo (21) to the north, Tavira (44) to the east, and Olhão (43) to the south. It is very easily reached by the EN270 which runs from Loulé through São Brás de Alportel and on to Tavira on the south coast.

Archaeology and Architecture
The Parish Church is in the centre of the town and has a 1931 clock tower and Renaissance doorways.

Landscape and Crops
The area is geologically very similar to São Brás de Alportel in that the northern part is Carboniferous slate and the southern part hard limestone with a narrow band of red sandstone in between, on which the

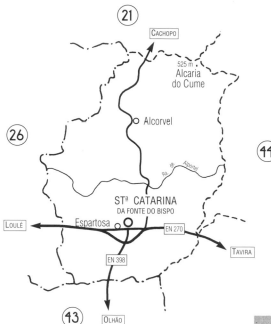

Almond, Fig and Carob Bean trees. A large number of Olive trees are found in places, some as much as 1,000 years old and still being used for the production of olive oil.

Fauna, Flora and Birdlife
Many of the hillsides are so steep as to make cultivation impossible. Here the Kermes Oak and Mastic Tree are the predominant shrub cover, with Gum, Narrow-leaved and Grey-leaved Cistus giving colour in the early part of the year. Many bulbous plants also add colour during spring, and Hoop-petticoat Narcissus, Barbary Nut, Spanish Iris, *Gladiolus byzantinus*, Grape Hyacinth, *Tulipa australis*, the huge-flowered *Scilla peruviana*,

town of Santa Catarina da Fonte do Bispo stands. This sandstone has broken down to form the clay used by the large number of brickyards in the area.

The highest point in the *freguesia* is at Alcaria do Cume (525m) on the dramatic and desolate moorland. Eucalyptus is grown where possible, and small patches of cereal land are sown and harvested where the soil is suitable. In the few river valleys, fertile soil provides good vegetables for local consumption. In the sandstone and limestone areas in the southern part of the *freguesia* many small fields divided by limestone walls are cultivated with cereals, while pasture land sustains

A typical scene – taking a well-earned rest after the daily chores in a quiet corner of a back-street in a small village surrounded by flowers and recently harvested produce. There are no panes of glass in the door windows which are shut in times of cold or wet weather. Note the broom made from the Dwarf Fan Palm.

Scilla monophyllos and the Spanish Bluebell all find nourishment between the rocks.

Many of the smaller birds frequent the cultivated ground, with flocks of House Sparrows, Linnets, and Goldfinches feeding in the cereal fields. During summer House Martins, swallows and swifts hunt insects near inhabited areas. In the hills, Kestrels, Buzzard, Booted and Bonelli's Eagles hunt for small rodents; the Short-toed Eagles prefer snakes.

Little Owls are seen in daytime on telephone wires and also perched on trees. This common small owl hunts mainly during early morning and evening, but may also be active during the day.

One of the spectacular moths of the Algarve, the Great Peacock, is the largest European moth, with a wing-span of up to 7cm. The 'eyes' on top of the fore and rear wings give a menacing appearance and offer some protection against predators. The caterpillars which can sometimes be found in gardens and orchards are huge and green with bright blue 'warts'.

Crafts and Local Produce

An important cooperative of olive oil producers has recently been modernised and can now be visited. It will soon have its own museum and direct sales department.

This is the most important area in southern Portugal for producing the *telhas*, *ladrilhos* and *tijolos* (roof tiles, floor tiles and hollow building bricks from clay) which are seen throughout the region, not only on outdoor terraces but in many cases as varnished floors within rustic-type houses.

Nineteen brickyards are spread along the red sandstone strip in the *freguesia*, where

Besides making these floor tiles which are used for outside terraces or varnished for indoor rustic flooring, traditional Roman-type roof tiles are also made in Santa Catarina da Fonte do Bispo. These graded, curved tiles were originally made on a man's thigh, before being dried and baked!

the clay is approximately 200m deep with a width of about 1km. At Espartosa on the EN270 west of Santa Catarina, José Celestino Martins' brickyard is around 70 years old. The clay is dug from around the factory and dried before being ground with a mill. Next, a 'Heath Robinson' machine mixes it with water into a thick paste (originally this was mixed by treading!), after which it is prepared like pastry and moulded by hand into slabs which are left to dry on the floor of the open-sided drying sheds. The

The beautiful caterpillar of the Striped Hawkmoth is common in the area. Most of the European hawkmoths are found in southern Portugal. Even the very rare Death's Head Hawkmoth caterpillar is occasionally seen feeding on jasmine or potato. The most common variety is the Hummingbird Hawkmoth.

'house mark' is three pale stripes, applied lengthways with fingers.

The tiles are dried for two days in summer and four to five in winter before firing in huge ovens at 900–1000°C for 30 hours. These ovens are fuelled with almond shells from the local almond-shelling plant at Santa Catarina da Fonte do Bispo. They give a fierce heat with very little smoke.

Pale grey clay comes from Loulé and mid-colour potter's clay from Tavira.

At the *Junta de Freguesia* details can be obtained of the *Associação Telheiros Artesanais* (the local tile producers).

Honey is collected in neighbouring villages and at Santa Catarina. Palm brushes and *empreita* work are also made in the area, along with baskets and wooden chairs with *tabua* (bulrush) seats.

SECTION 3
BAIXO ALENTEJO, MONCHIQUE AND COASTAL REGIONS

This section takes in all the adjacent areas to the north, south and west of the Caldeirão mountains.

Before 1966, the Algarve was a comparatively unknown area. The opening of a small airport in Faro in that year, however, prompted the massive changes and development which have transformed southern Portugal's fortunes. An increasingly large influx of tourists to the area was later accompanied by the opening of the 25 de Abril Bridge (originally the Salazar Bridge, but renamed after the revolution which toppled the dictator) across the River Tagus in Lisbon, which offered access to the south to both foreign tourists in Lisbon and the local population of the northern half of Portugal. Today, with the recent development of the new road network to the south, the popularity of the Algarve is likely to be maintained.

The southern Algarve tourist strip is nowhere more than 2km wide and has become an international conglomeration of modern buildings. Many are very attractive, but aside from a predilection for typical ornate chimneys, the new style of the Algarve has left little room for tradition.

Cows are still used for farm work in many parts of Portugal, especially in the west and in the mountainous areas in the north. Although they are slow they are immensely strong. They are very economic as they can also bring up a calf and provide milk for the home.

The problem is double-edged, for while the increased housing and, in particular, the vast number of golf-courses which have been developed both along the coast and, in some areas, further inland, have brought an improved standard of living, they have also irreversibly altered the ecosystems of the area. The windier west coast, on the other hand, has been declared a protected area and, thanks to more stringent building regulations, has by and large retained its charm. The community here might still be described as 'typically rural', but this in itself throws up the problem of earning a sufficient income for modern living.

The situation is not confined to the Algarve. The south-western Baixo Alentejo covers vast estates of purely agricultural land. Here the small villages, similar to those in the Caldeirão, are also dying, due to the exodus of the younger population, who leave in search of a better life elsewhere, many seeking it in the resorts of the Algarve. In the southern area of Monchique has attained a greater degree of self-sufficiency thanks to the beauty of the countryside and the development of tourist facilities. Its northern slopes are a different matter, and despite being considerably wetter than the south, they are experiencing similar problems to the Caldeirão.

28 ODEMIRA

This is the largest *concelho* in Portugal but only the southern part is covered by this book. It lies on the Atlantic coast and is bordered to the east by Ouriquc (29) and to the south by Aljezur (33) and Monchique (34). The town itself is well situated on the western EN120 route from Sagres and Lagos in the south to Alcácer do Sal, with the EN263 running to Aljustrel and Beja. Access to Monchique by the EN263, EN123 then EN266 is slow but picturesque. The EN393 road to Vila Nova de Milfontes and the west coast is just south of the town.

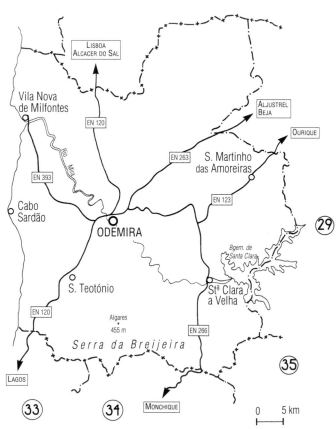

Archaeology and Architecture

The history of this area goes back to the Iron Age, relics of which have been found at the mouth of the Mira river. Approximately 90 years after its reconquest from the Arabs by the Knights Templar, the first charter was granted by Dom Afonso III in 1256. Later, at the instigation of Dom João II, Milfontes became the port for Odemira in 1486, gaining a fort ordered by Dom Filipe II the following century, built between 1599 and 1602.

Landscape and Crops

Odemira is a pretty town with a particularly lovely cool, shady garden *Jardim da Fonte Férrea*, which is surrounded by large trees including Horse Chestnuts and Grevilleas. In this area the northern slopes of Serra de Monchique and Serra da Brejeira sweep down to the Atlantic coastline, culminating in spectacular cliffs at Cabo Sardão, where the convoluted mass has seemingly been frozen into immobility by the relentless pounding of the sea. The highest point of 455m is in Serra da Brejeira at Algares. To preserve this environmentally important area the whole coastline has been designated a protected region.

The River Mira rises in the Serra do Caldeirão and forms the important reservoir of Santa Clara-a-Velha. Water from here is channelled through concrete canals, irrigating thousands of hectares of rich farming land for dairy cattle and flooding land suitable for rice production. Thanks to the ready availability of water a number of specialized horticultural enterprises have been developed. In the more mountainous regions to the south, large areas have been planted with Eucalyptus for wood pulp, but traditional farming methods continue in more isolated villages, where cows are often used for carting, ploughing and general farm work.

Fauna, Flora and Birdlife

In spring the countryside is a kaleidoscope of colour. Yellow is provided by the alien South African, Bermuda Buttercup which covers vast areas and is almost impossible to eradicate. The yellow of the Mimosas mixes with the red of the Pelargoniums planted by the roadsides by the *cantoneiros* (road builders). Pink and white heathers with Spanish and Dorset Heaths are widespread on some of the more acidic sandy areas and give a bright colour. Vivid blue comes in the form of the Shrubby Pimpernel, Scrambling Gromwell and Anchusa.

In the Mira river valley the moist conditions are ideal for dragonflies. Where the slightly acidic streams cut through the slate bedrock the Golden-ringed Dragonfly is

As soon as the rainy season begins, usually in October, fungi of many different species suddenly appear and some fields are full of mushrooms. There are many highly colourful fungi; *Gymnophyllus spectabilis* shown here is growing on felled Eucalyptus trees.

relatively common, and within the vegetated edges of the reservoir the Emperor and Lesser Emperor are common. The Beautiful Demoiselle and the Banded Demoiselle fly with species of blue damselflies.

Cork, Ilex and the semi-deciduous Lusitanian Oaks are widely grown, the annual prunings of the latter two being used to produce high-quality charcoal. Herds of the black Alentejano pigs can still be seen feeding on the acorns.

Crafts and Local Produce
In the town centre (and a little difficult to find) is the helpful tourist information office, which also displays local handicrafts.

Amilda Martins and Manuel Branco from Vale Bejinha make attractive original pottery, while baskets in willow and cane are made by José Jacinto Inácio and Vitorino José in Odemira. Maria Bárbara Alves weaves bags in linen, and Dona Arminda Guisanão embroiders pictures and works in false enamel. Cork chess boards with ceramic chessmen are made by one of the assistants at the tourist office.

On the eastern edge of town on the EN263 a marble factory has been producing everything from tiles to stairways, kitchen work-tops to gravestones for the past 25 years. Black marble comes from Beja and other colours from Estremoz in the central Alentejo. Granite, which is more expensive and more difficult to work, comes from Santa Eulalia further north. The marble is cut under running water with diamond saws, which cost about £300 but last for only six months (the diamond chisels used for carving cost around £100). Templates for lettering and crosses are made of very hard plastic.

São Martinho das Amoreiras has a craft *Cooperativa* called *Sonho Serrano*. Adelina Bárbara Vieira makes rag dolls, Maria da Silva knits intricate cotton table cloths and mats using five needles, and Mariana Gonçalves produces beautiful crochet work and weaving.

Beautiful crochet work is carried out throughout the region, in many cases using age-old designs. Besides the Odemira area there are a large number of artisans in the Alte (18) *freguesia* who also make beautiful work and can often be seen working outside in the shade.

STEPPE LANDS

29 OURIQUE, 30 CASTRO VERDE, 31 ALMODÔVAR AND PARTS OF 32 MÉRTOLA

The gently undulating plains of the Baixo Alentejo are typical steppe lands, consisting of grain-growing areas and large tracts of sparse grassland, and characterized by low rainfall, extremely hot summers and cool winters with frequent frosts. This land is within the *concelhos* of Ourique and Castro Verde, and the northern areas of Almodô-var and Mértola.

Landscape and Crops
The Alentejo is often called the 'granary of Portugal', and the plains near Castro Verde produce cereals and support large herds of cattle and sheep. The cattle are bred for meat, and the sheep for meat and wool, with their milk being turned into Serpa cheese.

Fauna, Flora and Birdlife
During the spring there is an ever changing colourful vista of white daisies, yellow marigolds, and lavender and pink Campion Catchfly. The white Gum and Narrow-leaved Cistus cover huge areas, while the *Rumex* colours the land red between Olive and oak trees. Jonquils, Hoop Petticoat Narcissus, Water Crowfoot and the

These arid areas of the Alentejo have a rich varied avifauna. Most spectacular is the Great Bustard, Europe's heaviest bird, with a fully grown male weighing more than 18kg. Extremely shy and vulnerable to habitat destruction, this species is on the endangered list.

Barbary Nut colour the banks of water courses. By June the grain is gathered and the soil is scorched tawny under a relentless sun. With the first rains of autumn the land bursts into green again.

Around 60 per cent of the Portuguese Great Bustard population is concentrated within the Castro Verde region. This highly protected species is the world's heaviest flying bird, with a mature male weighing more than 18kg. Its courtship display is a wonder of the ornithological world, since it appears to turn itself inside out (looking not dissimilar to a Parisian Can-can dancer!). Little Bustards are more widely distributed and more easily sighted, especially during the breeding season,

when the male's jet black neck can be seen poking up through scant vegetation as he guards his mate's nesting site.

The Stone Curlew, a crepuscular and shy bird, freezes and blends into the background on the approach of predators, with only its large bright eye giving it away. Black-bellied Sandgrouse are difficult to find, as they sit motionless during the mid-day heat. They are more likely to be spotted flying to drinking points in the early morning or evening.

Black and Red Kites are frequently seen, often scavenging on rubbish dumps or flying effortlessly over villages. Their beautiful relative, the Black-shouldered Kite, is much more local and recognized

There are many species of grasshoppers and crickets in southern Portugal, ranging from small ones barely a centimetre long to the migratory locust which is up to 6cm long. Some have red underwings, others blue. Body colour can range from bright green to brown, often depending on the stage of growth.

by its resemblance to the Kestrel. Its black shoulder and silver plumage are the diagnostic features.

In summer the visiting Montagu's Harrier is extremely common, usually seen quartering the land with great acrobatic agility while feeding on small mammals, birds or the mass of grasshoppers which inhabit this area. The rarer Hen Harrier is a winter visitor. Lesser Kestrels, which breed in Mértola, frequent the steppe lands during the daytime.

The Calandra Lark (Europe's largest lark), Bee-eater and Roller are often seen, the latter two – which are summer visitors – being possibly the most colourful of European birds. The resident Calandra Lark can easily be recognized by its large size and white trailing edge to the wings. White Storks are frequently sighted walking sedately in the short grassland in search of prey or congregating around water holes. They nest communally in trees, on telegraph poles or in specially constructed nesting sites. Singly they can be seen on church towers, disused windmills or chimneys. Spanish Sparrows often nest in the lower layers of the enormous nests.

29 OURIQUE

Ourique lies in the north of the area covered and is bounded by Santana da Serra (01) and Gomes Aires (02) to the south, Castro Verde (30) to the east, and Odemira (28) to the west. It is well situated on the main Albufeira to Lisbon motorway and the eastern EN123 to Castro Verde and Mértola, with its western continuation to Garvão and Monchique.

Archaeology and Architecture

This very old city, with its houses between one and two hundred years old, is steeped in history and well worth exploring. In the town centre is the Largo de Dom Dinis which has a clock tower and is surrounded by ancient buildings. A statue here commemorates Dom Dinis and his granting of the city charter on 8 January 1290 (reaffirmed by Dom Manuel in 1510).

The Castelo de Orik, set at the highest point in the town, was built in 711 by the Arabs. The walkways around the castle offer fantastic views over the southern Alentejo plains. In the adjoining gardens the

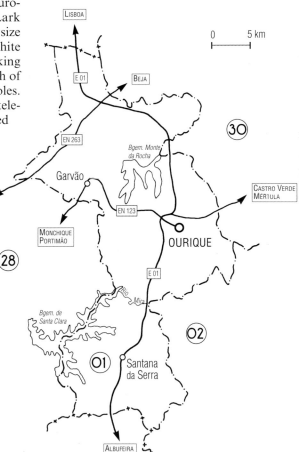

This high point in the Alentejo plains, just to the south-east of Castro Verde, is known as São Pedro das Cabeças and is the reputed site of the Battle of Ourique. It is strategically placed with a spectacular panoramic view over sparsely wooded grain and pasture land.

statue of Dom Afonso Henriques (the first king of Portugal, known as Dom Afonso I) commemorates his ousting of the Moors on 25 July 1139 at the Battle of Ourique (the probable site of which is in the Castro Verde *concelho*, 30). The 17th-century Hospital da Misericórdia retains its decorative stonework around the doorways and windows to this day. It still shows the stonemason's inscriptions from the time when it was done.

Crafts and Local Produce

Within the town the *artesanato* shop of *A Roca* ('The Distaff') also runs a successful weaving business, working with linen, cotton or rags, the latter used mainly for making rustic rugs. Ana do Patrocínio Sobral Penedo, who owns the shop, also made the three woven city shields for the

Town Hall, local treasury office and Hospital da Misericórdia.

Linen has been part of Portuguese culture since the 15th century and, although on the decline due to new man-made fibres, still features strongly throughout the region. Many remote areas continue with the old methods of its production. The seed is usually sown during April and the flax is pulled from the end of June. The fibres are then beaten to break open the stems, after which they are submerged in a river to begin the rotting process. They are left there for fifteen days before being dried for twelve days in an airy outdoor location. The outer stems are then crushed and the fibres separated, combed with a wooden 'comb' with metal teeth and spun, made into skeins and rolled into balls for use.

Carding wool is men's work. The cards weigh 2–2½kg each. This heavy work can cause crippling of the hands in later life. Wool is carded colour by colour or when mixed produces an in-between colour. On the right are piles of carded wool.

30 CASTRO VERDE

Castro Verde lies in the north and is bounded by Ourique (29) to the west, Mértola (32) to the east, and Almodôvar (04) and São Miguel do Pinheiro (07) to the south. It is easily reached by the EN123 from Ourique to Mértola, or the EN2 Faro to Lisbon road.

Archaeology and Architecture

Dom Manuel granted Castro Verde its charter in 1510. Today the town is dominated by the huge 18th-century Basilica Real church, built on the site of an old temple. Its magnificent *azulejos* panels depict the Battle of Ourique, before which the first king of Portugal, Dom Afonso Henriques, is purported to have seen a vision of Christ. The Church dos Remédios was built at the beginning of the 17th century by Dom Filipe III on the site of a chapel built by Dom Afonso Henriques.

Within this *concelho* on the prominent flat 'table' point (245m) at São Pedro das Cabeças, the Battle of Ourique is alleged to have taken place, when Dom Afonso Henriques ousted the Moors on 25 July 1139. The event is commemorated by a small chapel overlooking the vast plains of the Baixo Alentejo.

Landscape and Crops

The mine of Neves Corvo, opened in January 1989, is the largest copper and tin mine in the European Community and has huge reserves. Within a year of opening it had extracted a million tons of ore!

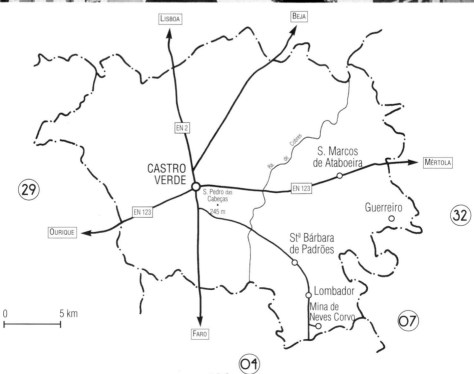

Castro Verde is an important town in the grain-growing Alentejo plains. The impressive *Basilica Real* dominates the old part of the town and can be seen for many kilometres around. One of the most important annual agricultural fairs of the region is held on the exhibition ground in October.

Fauna, Flora and Birdlife

This *concelho* typifies the wide open plain of the Baixo Alentejo and is ornithologically one of the most important areas in southern Portugal for steppe birds, most of which can be seen from the roadsides. White Storks are especially numerous, nesting on rooftops, trees or telegraph

There are many remote villages like this one, which is situated deep in the plains. Here the inhabitants rely on agriculture in one form or another, either tending large flocks of sheep and cattle or cultivating tracts of stony ground for thin crops of cereals.

poles, in particular at Monte dos Oliveiras on the Santa Bárbara de Padrões to Castro Verde road, where there are over forty nests on purpose-erected frames.

Crafts and Local Produce

In Lombador and other small villages the typical woollen blankets of the region are made according to age-old designs. The sheep are sheared by the men, and the ladies wash the wool in warm water and dry it in the fresh air, after which it is beaten with switches of Oleander wood to disentangle the fibres. Next it is put in large baskets and sprinkled with olive oil to make it soft. The carding is done by the men since the wood and metal cards weigh between 2kg–2.5kg each. Next the wool is spun and formed into skeins, which are washed to remove the oil and wound into balls ready for weaving on the rustic ancestral looms.

São Marcos da Ataboeira and Guerreiro are home to accomplished carpet and rug makers, who work the famous *ponto de Arraiolos* designs (from the town of Arraiolos just north of Évora) and many work under contract to Arraiolos. These carpets have become one of the principal crafts in Portugal and date back certainly to 1747, and probably to the beginning of the 17th century. The base is linen, jute, sacking or cotton and the intricate stitching, an oblique cross stitch, is pure wool with each stitch two threads wide by two or four long. The first stitch covers a double length with the cross over the bottom part only. This is repeated and the final effect is more like a plait than a cross-stitch! It must all be worked in lines otherwise the finished article would have a warped look. From beginning to end it is an intricate task of counting the stitches and following a paper pattern.

Several residents of these small villages are under contract to companies from Arraiolos to make the famous carpets of the region which are much in demand. Others still work on ancient looms making the traditional blankets from the local sheep's wool.

31 ALMODÔVAR

This northern part of the Almodôvar *concelho* is surrounded by Castro Verde (30) to the north, São Miguel de Pinheiro (07) and São Pedro de Solis (06) to the east, Santa Cruz (05) and Almodôvar (04) to the south, and Ourique (29) to the west. It covers a small area, the historical importance and natural history of which is detailed in the *freguesia* of Almodôvar and the steppe lands of Ourique (29) respectively.

Crafts and Local Produce

Cobbler Manuel Francisco Silvestre in Aldeia Fernandes is a craftsman to his fingertips! For years he has pursued a fascinating hobby in his spare time, studying and making miniature copies of 18th- and 19th-century shoes and boots. The smallest soles are 8cm long, with the largest 13cm. He has made original shoes which were 'two of a kind' with no distinction between left or right, shoes for ladies sickling in the fields, and smart black footwear for Sunday best. Likewise for men, he has

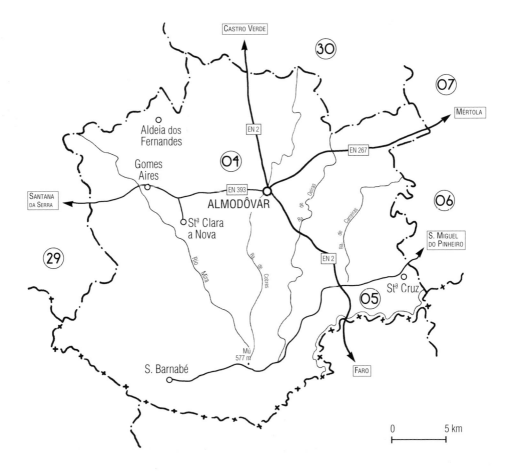

'My place in the sun' typifies many of these hamlets. In village squares there are usually one or two benches where the inhabitants can rest and enjoy the tranquillity away from the fast-moving modern-day life. More often than not, men are found here as the women have to attend to their household chores and cooking.

made heavy brown boots for work and black ones for Sunday and holidays. Beautiful boots with copper spurs for bullfighting, police boots, and boots for the army and marines all have their place in his collection of 42 pairs, plus a pair of leggings, donkey saddles, mule collars and even a miniature cartridge belt!

Each pair of boots is made in calf leather and stitched entirely by hand, and takes a minimum of six months to complete. Boots are the most difficult things for him to complete as it is impossible for him to get his hand inside to perform the perfect stitching, and he has to use pliers to pull through and re-insert the needle. The laced varieties are easier to make. The finished products are so evenly worked that they look as if they have been machine made.

Right This fireside table is filled with miniature shoes, which are a hobby of the cobbler! Each pair of these 18th- and 19th-century copies takes six months to make. In the very front is a pair of shoes where both are identical, as original shoes were made to fit either foot!

Above The Jonquil and Hoop-petticoat Narcissus growing profusely in a remote winter-flowing stream, with some clones of the latter a pale lemon yellow. The plants grow in a narrow strip on either side where the soil is continually wet during winter and spring.

32 MÉRTOLA

This is the most north-eastern *concelho* covered in this book, with several of its *freguesias* given special coverage. It is bounded by the border with Spain to the east, São Pedro de Solis (06), São Miguel de Pinheiro (07), São Sebastião dos Carros (08) and Espírito Santo (09) to the south, and Almodôvar (31) westwards. Mértola town is on an important crossroads, where the EN122 from Vila Real de Santo António to Beja on the south-eastern extremity of Portugal intersects with the EN265 to Serpa and the EN267 to Almodôvar.

Archaeology and Architecture

Viewed from its imposing castle, the town is a medley of roofs, tiny winding streets and important historic buildings. Because of its five museums – the Museu Islâmico, Museu de Arte Sacra, Museu Romano, Museu Paleocristão, and Forja do Ferreiro (Blacksmith's forge) – Mértola is considered a museum town.

For five centuries, Roman *Myrtilis* was important in terms of both agriculture and minerals, in particular gold from the São Domingos mine. Excavations during recent years have unearthed not only the Roman forum and an extremely well preserved cryptoporticum (which took five

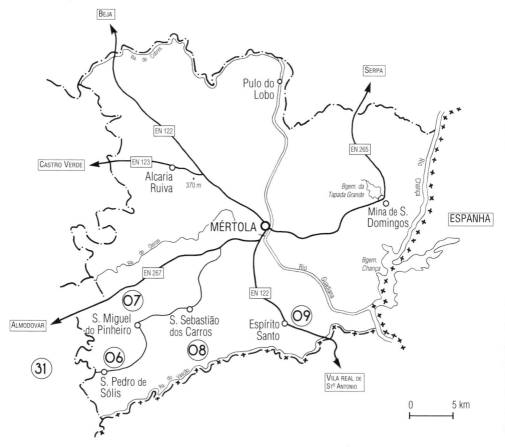

years to retrieve), but also the overlying Islamic remains, for the Arabs also left many monuments, some of which can still be seen.

During restoration of the elaborate Parish Church with its five naves at the beginning of the 20th century, a mihrab and minbar were discovered behind the altar, confirming that this was the original mosque from the 12th century. The city walls were erected in the 12th century with the construction of the castle following in the 13th century. The castle is considered the most impregnable in Western Iberia. The 17th century produced the Convent of São Francisco and the small chapel of the Calvary which were followed in the 18th century by the clock tower. An excellent pictorial book sold at the tourist office gives further details.

Landscape and Crops

This gently undulating *concelho* reaches its highest point of 370m near Alcaria Ruiva. The Rio Guadiana (famous for the strange, eel-like Lampreys which are culinary delicacies) passes through the centre of the *concelho* having entered the area in the north at Pulo do Lobo ('Wolf's Leap'), where it has cut a narrow, spectacular 2m wide gorge through the hard rock. It is joined at Mértola by the Ribeira de Oeiras. Most of the soil is arenaceous schist, dry and with many rocky outcrops, which makes cereal growing difficult. Sheep are extensively grazed, producing meat, fine wool and milk, which is processed into much-valued cheese.

From 1858 to 1965, Mason and Barry held the mining rights to the vast copper

The Rio Guadiana flows gently down to the sea passing by the impressive town hall in Mértola. During the great flood of 6–7 December 1876 this river rose to disastrous proportions and even reached the council square, but on retreating revealed many archaeological treasures.

and sulphur mine at São Domingos (the same one worked by the Romans), which employed 6,000 workers. From 1867 the ore was transported by rail to Pomarão (previously by mule-drawn wagons), then by boat to Vila Real de Santo António, from where it was exported to the United Kingdom and the Americas.

Fauna, Flora and Birdlife
During spring the large expanses of colourful flora give rise to ever-changing vistas which are well worth seeing. The birdlife of the area is also interesting. In autumn, numbers of Griffon and Black, with occasional Egyptian Vultures, are often seen spiralling in the sky on the southern migration, and throughout the year Great and Little Bustards are frequently observed from the roadsides. All these are strictly protected, as are White Storks which nest in Mértola town and on

telegraph poles on the road to Castro Verde (the bases of the latter nests inhabited by large numbers of Spanish Sparrows during their breeding season). In late spring, Montagu's Harriers and Black and Red Kites perform aerial acrobatics in their search for food in the countryside. Over the castle and convent in Mértola, Lesser Kestrels are always in evidence during the summer months, hawking for insects and looking like large swallows. They nest in holes in the castle walls or in specially provided nest boxes. During the day, many of these birds frequent the steppe lands. In the eastern valleys with rocky cliffs the large Eagle Owl is heard but rarely seen.

In the early 1900s, Wolves were relatively common, but had become extinct in the region by 1920. Wild Boar are, however, still numerous and occasionally need to be culled under licence.

White Storks feeding on the Alentejo pasture lands. These majestic birds feed exclusively on live animal matter such as small mammals, lizards, frogs, snails and a large number of locusts and grasshoppers. They are often seen wandering round rubbish dumps feeding on mice and insects.

Crafts and Local Produce

Along with many areas of the Baixo Alentejo and the districts of Almodôvar (04) and Castro Verde (30) in particular, Mértola is famous for its traditional woollen blankets, the designs and natural colours of which have been used for hundreds of years. Realizing that the craft was declining rapidly, the town established a school to train people in the arts of carding, spinning and weaving, and now it has a flourishing cooperative which specializes in these traditionally designed brown and white blankets using the *montanhac* (diamond shapes), *espiga* (ears of wheat) and various stripes and checks.

Beautiful jewellery is made in the *Museu de Arte Sacra,* one of five museums in this historic town. Many of the designs are replicas of old designs, but others are original with Roman and Arab influences.

It is not really surprising that a jewellery business, housed in the Museu de Arte Sacra and using age-old designs, has also been started in this town. Following a three-year course, three young ladies now make replicas of some of the pieces found during the excavation of local sites, as well as originals based on Roman and Arabic designs. The jewellery is worked in copper, brass or silver, with gold pieces made to order.

33 ALJEZUR

Aljezur is another 'forgotten' area, bounded by the Atlantic to the west, Odemira (28) to the north, Monchique (34) and Lagos (37) to the east, and Vila do Bispo (36) at the most south-western point. The EN120 Lagos to Alcácer do Sal road passes through the area and minor roads lead to the coast and the Monchique mountain range.

Archaeology and Architecture

Aljezur's history goes back to Arab times in the 10th century, when the now ruined castle was built. In the old terraced town are remnants of a pillory, probably from the 15th century, and the Misericórdia Church, which was built in the 16th century and completely reconstructed in the 18th century, when the Parish Church was also built. The remains of 15th-century fortifications can be seen at Arrifana and vestiges of other buildings at Odeceixe. The Parish Church of Bordeira has a Manueline portal from the 15th century, but is mainly an 18th-century building with beautifully carved and gilded woodwork.

Landscape and Crops

This *concelho* sweeps down from the western foothills of Monchique with the slate and shale ending abruptly at the coastline in high and often rugged cliffs. Carrapateira, Amoreira and Odeceixe have wide sandy beaches where small rivers empty into the Atlantic. Many of the estuaries and clifftops are shaped by extensive sand dune systems which support unique flora. This delicate ecosystem is now a protected landscape within the Sudoeste Alentejano e Costa Vicentina. Fossils exposed in rocks underlying the sand range from well preserved corals dating from the early

Along the high cliffs fishermen stand precariously on the very edge with the raging sea 100m below. Sea bream and bass are the main fish caught in the deep water just offshore. Very long home-made rods are often used, made from local bamboo.

nosae, mainly *Ononis natrix*, the Large Yellow Restharrow. *Cistus palhinhae* and *crispus* cover large areas with white or pink flowers along with the curious *Corema album*, which is only found on an Atlantic dune habitat.

The large and usually quite rare Ribbon-tailed Lacewing is found during April and May flitting from plant to plant.

The hillsides on the Monchique watershed are covered with Gum Cistus, Tree Heather and Lusitanian Heath. Many areas of thin soil are planted with Eucalyptus and pines for timber, with some Maritime Pines being tapped for resin and Umbrella Pines used for dune stabilization near Bordeira.

Otters inhabit the river valleys at Carrapateira and Aljezur and the Egyptian Mongoose is common.

Migrating bird movement can be spectacular, especially in autumn (during one September afternoon more than 400 Booted Eagles were counted).

Around Aljezur small herds of goats and sheep feed on the hillsides, where some cork is harvested. Grapes, fruit and market crops grow in the valleys, and on the sandy plateau near Rogil wheat and maize are cultivated with a large quantity of groundnuts. Aljezur is known for its Sweet Potatoes (*batata doce*), for which this area is considered by many to be the finest in Portugal. On the coast of Pontal vast amounts of red fan-shaped seaweed are collected by divers and sold to Lisbon for the manufacture of agar-agar and other pharmaceutical products.

Miocene period (16 million years ago) to Terebratulidae bivalves from the Jurassic period (160 million years ago).

Fauna, Flora and Birdlife
Many rare plants grow in the sand dunes, including *Antirrhinum major*, the ancestor of the cultivated Snapdragon, which winds its way with tendrils through the scrubby undergrowth, and large spectacular Broomrape parasite species of Legumi-

Crafts and Local Produce
Crafts are not high on the list of occupations; there are a few basket makers who work with locally grown willow, and crochet work can often be seen. Francisco António from Rogil makes decorative outdoor lights from plaster of Paris and cement, some in

The Large Yellow Restharrow is a common and beautiful Leguminous (Pea family) plant usually growing in the form of a mound, often having species of *Orobanche* living on it parasitically. The introduced Century Plant with its tree-like inflorescence is in the background.

the form of chimneys, and brass and copper goods are made in Aljezur.

Aljezur is also home to two of Portugal's most renowned ceramic artists, who run their own gallery here, *Manusfactum*. Ernesto Silva and his wife Zabel Moita were both born in Aljezur and since 1987 have exhibited ceramics both in Portugal and abroad with enormous success. (They are also both notable poets who have won national prizes, and Sra Zabel collects and publishes traditional recipes.) Originally they dug clay for their ceramics locally, dried it in the sun and mixed it with water. Now they obtain it from the north. The pieces they make are unique and the techniques they employ individual, and their

work is all designed and fired at their home. Occasionally a wheel is used for turning, but most of the smaller items are made using home-made instruments. (Sr. Ernesto makes templates from vegetables or fruit for marking moist clay.) Once articles are moulded, they are left to dry for 10–15 days before being fired at a temperature of 1200°C for eight or nine days. After cooling the pieces are painted.

Sr. Ernesto uses infusions of seeds and leaves for colour, giving an impression of beautifully carved walnut or rich maho-

gany. His wife often uses unusual, delicate shades of pink, lilac and grey. After painting, the models are once again baked at 350°C to set the final colour.

Sr. Ernesto prefers to create stylized animals, reptiles and birds inspired by the surrealism of Hieronymus Bosch, with some pieces up to 60cm high.

Sra. Zabel concentrates on people and her extraordinary theological models of 'The Last Supper' or 'The Nativity', which are up to 50cm wide, show incredible detail and skill.

On the left-hand side of the picture is one of Zabel Moita's figurines with Ernesto Silva's surrealistic work next to it. This renowned couple exhibit throughout Portugal and Spain with remarkable success and run their own gallery, *Manusfactum*, in Aljezur.

34 MONCHIQUE

Monchique is a mountainous *concelho* bordered by Odemira (28) to the north, São Marcos da Serra (10) to the east, Silves

(35), Portimão (38) and Lagos (37) south-wards, and Aljezur (33) to the west. The winding EN266 from Portimão on the south coast wends its way north through Monchique before dividing at Luzianes for Odemira or Ourique. South of Monchique town the picturesque road from Nave and Marmelete leads to Aljezur.

Archaeology and Architecture
Monchique's smaller neighbour, Caldas de Monchique, is a typical spa town with leafy squares and Victorian-style buildings. The

Throughout the region Manueline art is in evidence. This side door in the Parish Church, with the main doorway, are excellent examples of this flamboyant style, which was prevalent in the late 15th and early 16th centuries. Jerónimos Monastery in Lisbon and the famous window in Tomar are perhaps the most well-known examples.

Romans frequented the mineral springs here, bathing in the waters which emerge at a constant temperature of 32°C. Monchique itself is a hilly town 7km to the north, best explored on foot. The 16th-century Parish Church shows to perfection its two Manueline doorways, while the churches of São Sebastião and Misericórdia have interesting 17th- and 18th-century interiors. The Chapel of Senhor do Pé da Cruz dates from the 17th century, as does the Convent of Nossa Senhora do Desterro (Our Lady of Exile), which sadly has been allowed to fall into excessive decay. Its imposing shell dominates the heights above the town and is well worth the scramble up a pathway for the magnificent views over the *serra*.

Alferce's small church is worth a visit in passing, and so too are the Parish Church and Chapel of Santo António in Marmelete.

Landscape and Crops
The road to Marmelete offers breathtaking views to the coast. Foia, the highest point in southern Portugal (902m), and neighbouring Picota (773m) have the highest annual average rainfall in the region at 1,200mm. The Monchique massif is a syenite intrusion with acidic soil (pH5.5) between the granite boulders scattered over the mountainside. On the periphery, where small villages are dotted, Carboniferous slate predominates.

Fauna, Flora and Birdlife
This Mediterranean habitat with a strong Atlantic influence and high rainfall is botanically extremely rich. Oranges, cherries, peaches and chestnuts grow on the terraced hillsides, but these give way to a treeless heath near the summit with areas of the rare *Rhododendron ponticum* ssp. *baeticum*, *Paeonia broteroi* and the Dense-flowered

The spectacular *Rhododendron ponticum* subspecies *baeticum* is very restricted in its range as it is only found locally on the Serra de Monchique, further north in the Serra do Caramulo, and on one mountain in Andalucia. It is possibly a relic of the preglacial period.

Many areas unsuitable for traditional economic production have been terraced for planting of pines, or the rapid growing eucalyptus for wood pulp production. Eucalyptus is logged at ten years. This cutting activates the dormant adventitious buds into growth and additional felling occurs in a further ten years.

the semi-deciduous Lusitanian Oak, which is good for producing charcoal.

The present tree cover is primarily Cork Oak, pine and large plantations of Eucalyptus grown for wood pulp. The Strawberry Tree (also found in Ireland), with an undergrowth of predominantly Gum, Salvia- and Poplar-leaved varieties of cistus, grows between the cork and pine trees. The rare *Drosophyllum lusitanicum* and Broad-leaved Helleborine are found in grassy areas, while the roadsides are lined with Mimosa, which flowers at its best during February.

Birds found in the woodlands include woodpeckers and tits, including the Crested Tit. Azure-winged Magpies and warblers can be seen in the valleys, and in the summertime there are also cuckoos and Nightingales. During the autumn migration eagles and vultures pass overhead. The moist valleys with permanent streams harbour dragonflies, especially the Golden-ringed, which prefers these acidic woodland streams for breeding. Thanks to the large

Orchid, the latter also found in the Burren in western Ireland on limestone. The original tree cover was Canary Oak and Lusitanian Oak, with the Cork Oak arriving at a later date. This ancient afforestation has almost disappeared except for a few places on the northern slopes where you still find

quantity of Strawberry Trees the Two-tailed Pasha butterfly is common, as is the large Woodland Grayling.

Crafts and Local Produce
This is a productive area, with huge syenite quarries at Nave, where you can also watch men by the roadside fashioning granite cubes for paving stones. Cork is an important crop – after the bark is removed any prunings are used for excellent quality charcoal. *Medronho*, the local firewater, is made from the fruit of the Strawberry Tree, and honey is collected in the surrounding maquis area.

Artisan shops can be found in Caldas de Monchique, Monchique and at Foia. Basket making is still carried on with willow, and wooden spoons are diligently made using the hard, smooth wood of the Strawberry Tree. Old methods for spinning and weaving are still employed, starting with the locally grown flax being immersed in first hot and then cold water for ten days, to induce the rotting of unwanted material and leave the essential fibres. A metal-edged piece of wood is then used to render the fibres, after which they are combed. Having spun the threads, they are whitened by boiling in a mixture of water, wood ash, and a little coarse local blue and white soap, a different method from that described in Ourique (29).

One of the most interesting crafts seen here is the production of *cadeiras de tesoura* ('scissor chairs'). The scissor design dates from Roman times, when the chairs were much more elaborate, often incorporating lion head motifs. They have been made in Monchique for many decades, originally to order for wealthy homes. They take roughly four hours to make. Alder, growing in wetter mountain areas, is used, as it is comparatively fast growing. Previously it was Sweet Chestnut which lasts longer, but is now rapidly diminishing.

35 SILVES

Silves is bordered by São Marcos da Serra (10), São Bartolomeu de Messines (17) and Albufeira (40) to the east, Lagoa (39) to the south, Portimão (38) to the west, and Monchique (34) to the north. It is situated on the EN124 to Barranco do Velho and Alcoutim in the east and EN124-1 to Lagoa and Carvoeiro in the south.

Archaeology and Architecture
The town of Silves, one-time capital of the Algarve, is dominated by its well preserved red sandstone castle, the origin of which is uncertain. There was probably some sort of settlement here when the Romans arrived, since they took this as their headquarters and built fortifications. Later, the Arabs made it their capital, before they were conquered by the Knights of the Order of Santiago in the 13th century. Today the castle certainly warrants a visit.

The Gothic style 13th–14th-century cathedral was built on the site of a mosque and has been renovated several times, most recently between 1931 and 1955. The 16th-century Misericórdia Church has a Manueline side door, while the bridge was probably built during the 13th century on the site of its Roman predecessor. Another interesting feature of this historic town is the Cruz de Portugal, situated under a protective cupola on Silves' eastern boundary. This cross could be said to be Gothic in style, and has Manueline motifs and symbols. Many think it might date from the time of Dom João I (1385–1483). Its name, the 'Cross of Portugal', indicates that it was probably brought from the centre or north of the country when the Algarve was considered to be a separate kingdom.

One other point of note in this borough is the bone chapel at Alcantarilha, which adjoins the Parish Church.

The castle at Silves with its impregnable dark red sandstone battlements withstood countless attacks. It stands protectively above the modern town and overlooks the Arade river, which was navigable by caravels at the time of the discoveries but is now impeded by decades of heavy silting.

Landscape and Crops

The geology of the remainder of Silves *concelho* covers a wide range of ecosystems. On the coastal strip at Armação de Pêra alluvium and sands with sedimentary

154

gravel predominate. With their high content of iron oxides they give the soil a rich orange colour. Inland from the coast a series of low limestone hills forms a large part of the unique area known as *barrocal*, rich in botanical gems and with intensively cultivated farmland in the valleys producing olives, almonds, figs, oranges, maize and grapes. This is the centre of the Algarve's orange growing industry. The deep red

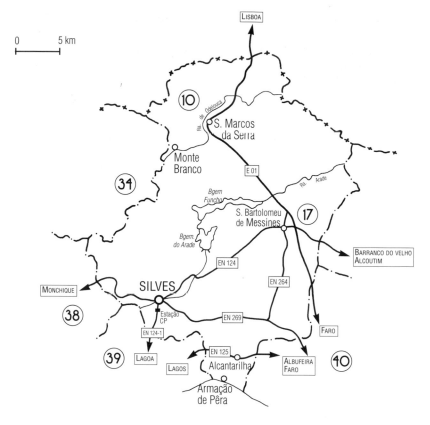

sandy soil is well irrigated from the Barragem de Arade and the relatively sheltered valley gives ideal conditions.

The town of Silves lies on the strip of Triassic sandstone which forms the transition area between the dolomitic limestone hills of the south and the Carboniferous shale–slate hills to the north. The hills to the north are covered with cistus scrub and plantations of Eucalyptus and pines. The indigenous Cork Oak produces bark that sustains the various cork-processing factories in the area.

Fauna, Flora and Birdlife
The orchards of the area are home to Golden Orioles during the summer, as well as a large number of finches, warblers and

flocks of Waxbill which were introduced from Africa during the 1960s. In the hills birds of prey can be seen riding the thermals, especially during the migratory periods. The deep 'oohoo' of the huge Eagle Owl can often be heard at dawn and dusk during spring.

The Pardel Lynx has been reported during recent years, and Genets and Egyptian Mongoose are frequent in the wilder maquis areas around the reservoir.

The Crab Spider lies in wait in the centre of a flower for unsuspecting flies or bees, which it grasps with its strong fore-legs. Although only 1cm long it attacks insects many times its size and its lethal venom is so potent that death is almost instantaneous. It is harmless to humans!

156

Crafts and Local Produce

Silves is the only borough in southern Portugal where children are taught the art of bobbin lace from the age of six. Near Silves station attractive tiles and pottery are made by *Roda Viva*. Good quality cork (*amadia*) comes from the third and successive strippings of a Cork Oak trunk, and is used for making bottle stoppers – it is fascinating to watch Domingos Ricardo dos Santos from Monte Branco making corks with only a knife and manually operated lathe called a *garlopa*. Squares of cork are firmly secured and then rapidly revolved against a blade to shape them. Domingos produces one thousand corks in an hour!

Towards Alcantarilha from Silves a large cork factory produces boards, mainly for insulation. Poor quality *virgem* cork is crushed with huge metal rollers to produce granules. Blocks are made by packing these granules into large containers and compressing. Autoclaving at a temperature of 360°C fuses the granules together. They are then cooled under running water at a temperature of 80°C before being kept separate for a further two hours to cool, after which they are stacked. A period of eight days 'resting' is necessary before these blocks are cut into sheets of varying thickness.

Granules are also sold to be spread on oil slicks at sea as they absorb petroleum.

Silves is a *concelho* where cork products are an important part of the economy. The main industries are insulation boards and Champagne corks for France, but local people still make corks and cork mats. Here the hand-operated *garlopa* is being used to produce 1,000 corks hourly.

36 VILA DO BISPO

This most south-westerly district of Europe is bounded by the Atlantic Ocean to the west and south, Aljezur (33) to the north and Lagos (37) to the east. It is situated at the end of the EN125 which traverses the south coast, joining the EN268 western route from Cabo de São Vicente and Sagres towards Lisbon. This entire coastline lies within the nature reserve of Sudoeste Alentejano e Costa Vicentina, which was created to preserve the region's unique flora, habitats and beauty.

Archaeology and Architecture

Megaliths between Vila do Bispo and Sagres offer evidence of prehistoric occupation, and vestiges of Roman and Phoenician settlements can also be seen. The most notable of these is located at Boca do Rio, where time has eroded a considerable part of a once impressive villa, but it still has remnants of mosaic flooring and fish-salting pans. At Martinhal, recent excavations have revealed kilns used for producing amphorae in which preserved fish were transported to Rome. Coins found here date the site from between the 2nd and 5th

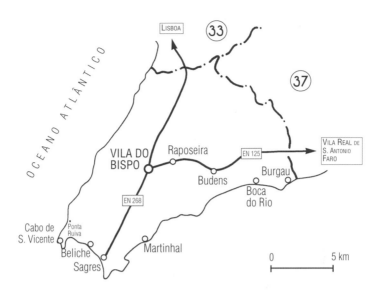

centuries, with many wells and irrigation systems stemming from Moorish times.

The area is architecturally interesting, with Raposeira's 13th-century chapel of Nossa Senhora de Guadalupe credited to the Knights Templar, and 17th-century features in the São Lourenço Chapel and Parish Church at Budens. The fortress at Beliche near Cabo de São Vicente is from the same era but also has vestiges of older

The Shrubby Violet is very local in distribution and is only found here at Cabo de São Vicente and at Cape Trafalgar in southern Spain. The Sagres peninsula has many endemic plants. During most of the year it is a colourful rock garden most of us would be proud to own, and is at its best from March to June.

159

buildings, while Sagres has the 15th-century Nossa Senhora da Graça church and 16th-century fortress (modified in 1756). Also here, of course, is the famous compass rose which is probably from the time of Henry the Navigator in the 15th century, since his school of navigation was situated just inside the fortress walls. Vila do Bispo's beautiful 18th-century church is well known for its classic blue and white *azulejos* and decorative fresco paintings of the nave vault. Both Burgau and Boca do Rio have ruined forts on the high limestone cliffs.

Due to its strategic position, the prominent lighthouse at Cabo de São Vicente (74 steps to the top!) houses the most important and largest light in Europe for marine and aircraft navigation. Henry the Navigator lived in the small castle on the right of the lighthouse grounds, as is testified by the Royal Coat of Arms carved in stone over the doorway. The slits on either side of this were for the draw-bridge.

Fauna, Flora and Birdlife

At Cabo de São Vicente the hard dolomitic limestone culminates in dramatic, 100m high cliffs. Sand has filled fissures and cracks on top of the rocks, forming anchorage for a multitude of plants in this wild and windswept landscape. Many endemic plants thrive, the most noticeable being *Cistus palhinhae* which dominates large areas, along with *Biscutella vincentina*, *Scilla vincentina* and *Linaria algarviana*. The Shrubby Violet and *Iris filifolia* are found locally, as well as spectacular mounds of strongly scented *Thymus camphoratus*. Brilliant clumps of Shrubby Pimpernel line the roadsides, while the very spiny *Astragalus massiliensis* is prolific in the fissured limestone around Sagres. The Triassic sandstone which traverses the Algarve and divides the *barrocal* limestone from the Carboniferous slate reaches the western coastline at Ponta Ruiva just north of Cabo de São Vicente. It is along this sand-

stone strip that most of the settlements are situated, including Vila do Bispo, Raposeira and Budens.

On the slate and shale, the vegetation changes and is more reminiscent of the Alentejo. Maritime Pine and plantations of Eucalyptus are dominant, with almonds and figs cultivated near villages.

Sagres peninsula, where fishermen sit impossibly close to the edge of the cliffs dangling their lines in the depths below, is a

The lighthouse at Cabo de São Vicente (known as 'The End of the World' in the Middle Ages) is framed by the endemic *Cistus palhinhae* in the foreground and the imported Hottentot Fig as ground cover. This cistus is closely related to the Gum Cistus but lacks the purple spot in the petals, is shorter and has stickier leaves.

mecca for bird watchers. Swifts, Shags and Choughs breed on the cliffs while vast numbers of Gannets migrate along the coastline. Booted Eagles, Griffon and Egyptian Vultures, Black and White Storks pass over in quantity during the autumn migration, and in spring this is the first landfall for notable numbers of Golden Orioles, Nightingales, Black-eared Wheatears and many other passerines and waders.

Boca do Rio (where Genets and Badgers have been seen in recent years) has a number of Otters and Egyptian Mongoose, and Wild Boar inhabit woodlands to the north of the region.

Apart from the horticulture usually associated with village life, most land is poor pasture used for grazing cattle, sheep and goats or cultivated for thin cereal crops.

Crafts and Local Produce

Boat building is still practised in Sagres down by the harbour, where the fishing fleet off-loads its catch, and there is usually a skeletal boat frame in view.

Again, throughout this region, crafts are not of great significance, but just inside the gates of the lighthouse at Cabo de São Vicente you'll find the most south-westerly artisan group in Europe! Five ladies (wives of the lighthouse keepers) can be found crocheting here on weekdays. Bootees, table mats, pin cushions and attractive soap holders are on offer, all in white with cheerful coloured decoration. In addition, *artesanato* shops are scattered throughout the region, mostly selling goods from more northern areas of the country.

Some fishermen climb precariously down the steep cliffs (their lives often dependent upon companions waiting by the safety ropes) to collect Goose Barnacles from the rock face. These *percebes* are considered a great delicacy.

The most south-westerly artisans' group in Europe is found just inside the gates of the lighthouse at Cabo de São Vicente. Here several ladies, wives of the five lighthouse keepers, sit and work at their delightful bright and colourful crochet souvenirs.

37 LAGOS

Lagos *concelho* is bordered by the Atlantic to the south, Portimão (38) to the east, Monchique (34) and Aljezur (33) to the north, and Vila do Bispo (36) to the west. It is strategically situated on the west–east EN125 along the coast, at the start of the western EN120 through Aljezur, Odemira and Santiago do Cacém to Grãndola and Alcácer do Sal.

Archaeology and Architecture

Lagos has always played a part in Portuguese history. Dolmen caves a little further inland in the Portimão (38) region indicate that it was probably inhabited 5,500 years ago, and the small Ribeira de Bensafrim was of economic use when the Phoenicians were here 3,000 years ago. The Greeks used the port on their voyages of trade, and they were followed by the Celts and Romans (the latter called it *Lacobriga*, which accounts for many of the local names within the town). The Moors knew the area as Zawaia, and when they were driven out in the 13th century it became Lagos.

Portugal's great Voyages of Discovery left from here and Lagos was also the site of the first ever slave sale, which was held in a field in 1444. The purpose-built slave market which came afterwards is now a small exhibition centre.

The town walls date from the 16th century and the Porta da Bandeira Fort from the 17th century. A small Manueline window overlooking the gardens along the busy Avenida now belongs to the hospital. The dual-carriageway Avenida dos Descobrimentos was opened in 1960 to commemorate the 500th anniversary of the death of Henry the Navigator. In 1960 this was an ambitious project, but with the coming of modern tourism it showed very good foresight.

Monuments are in abundance in Lagos: the Igreja de Santo António, with its incredible gilding and 18th-century *azulejos*, is commonly known as the Gold Church, and often approached from the adjoining municipal museum. The 16th-century Church of Santa Maria is also worth a visit.

A number of outlying villages in this *concelho* are also of note, in particular Odiáxere, where the church was reconstructed after the 1755 earthquake but still has its red sandstone Manueline portal. At Ponta da Piedade there are remnants of a medieval monastery.

Landscape and Crops

Spectacular high cliffs dominate the wide, sandy beaches of the coastline. Westwards from the rock formations and grottoes at Ponta da Piedade, high cliffs of Cretaceous limestone and sandstone stretch as far as Praia da Luz, where the basalt (volcanic) outcrop popularly known as 'Black Rock' forms a dramatic landmark. Inland the limestone ends abruptly in high escarpments near Bensafrim, which lies on the red sandstone. The land to the north is Carboniferous slate. Both rivers of Lagos *concelho* rise in the Serra de Espinhaço do Cão, the Bensafrim emptying into the sea at Lagos and the Odiáxere feeding the Bravura reservoir, reaching the sea east of Meia Praia.

Fauna, Flora and Birdlife

Plant life is spectacular on the limestone during spring, with an abundance of orchids on the hillsides. Many of the insect mimicry orchids are found near Bensafrim, along with a profusion of Pyramidal Orchids up until early June. Here you can also find *Scilla peruviana* in moist areas. In mid-winter *Iris planifolia* grows in quantity in the deep red limestone soil near Lagos, before the Almond blossom transforms the landscape.

Higher land north of the dam is heavily wooded with indigenous Cork Oak and an undergrowth of cistus species, as well as Kermes Oak, Strawberry Tree and in moist ground Blackberry bushes. Large areas are also planted with Eucalyptus. Nightingales can often be found around Blackberry

The very unusual Ribbon-tailed Lacewing is an uncommon insect of southern Portugal, closely related to the Ant Lion family. It is easily recognized by its hind wings, which are modified into the form of a feather, enabling the insect to hover over flowers and there catch the small insects on which it feeds.

bushes, and this sort of habitat in general is ideal for Wild Boar and Red Fox.

As in similar areas with the Strawberry Tree, the Two-tailed Pasha butterfly is often seen. Other butterflies which are frequently sighted include the Adonis and Common Blues, Swallowtail and Scarce Swallowtail, and early in the season the Spanish Festoon. There have also been rare sightings of the American Painted Lady and Lorquin's Blue.

Birds are numerous: White Storks nest on the high chimneys of the disused sardine factories in Lagos, and near Ponta da Piedade, 400 pairs of Cattle and Little Egrets nest on off-shore stacks, with Jackdaws and Rock Doves in the surrounding cliffs. Cormorants also winter here in quantity. In woodlands, gregarious Azure-winged Magpies feed on acorns, and Jays and Green and Great Spotted Woodpeckers are common. Wintering Ospreys often fish in the Bravura reservoir.

Crafts and Local Produce

Odiáxere has a typical monthly market where farmers sell livestock, fruit and seeds as well as a few locally made artefacts.

Helder Francisco Rodrigues Castanho in Lagos specializes in batik pictures of traditional fishing boats. Batik is the art of dyeing fabrics using wax to prevent the dyes from penetrating specific areas. Archaeological evidence shows that this ancient art dates back to over 2,000 years ago in the Far East, although the name didn't originate until the 12th century in Java. The technique was introduced to Europe by the Portuguese and Dutch in the 17th century.

Traditional marzipan sweetmeats are made from Lagos through Portimão (38) and Estômbar in the Lagoa *concelho* (39), with Lagos holding an annual exhibition towards the end of July. The paste, made with ground almonds, sugar, egg whites

Vegetable and fruit markets with the adjoining fresh fish market are fascinating. This recently constructed light and airy market is in uptown Lagos, with the 1924 riverside one still in use. Some are just half a dozen street stalls, as in Alte. Olhão and Lagoa have century-old markets, but all have their own particular magic.

and often lemon juice, vanilla and almond essence, is shaped into delicately coloured fruit, vegetables and on occasion elaborate 'sculptures'.

Another speciality is Dom Rodrigos, which you'll see sold in silver paper. These consist of ground almonds beaten into a thick syrup of sugar, water and egg yolks, and encased in *fios de ovos* – fine threads of egg yolk dropped through a funnel into boiling syrup. They are cooked in syrup and allowed to cool before wrapping.

38 PORTIMÃO

Portimão lies on the southern coastline and is bounded by Lagos (37) to the west, Lagoa (39) and Silves (35) to the east, and Monchique (34) to the north. The EN125 passes through the town, with the new bridge and bypass slightly to the north. The EN266 to Monchique gives easy access to the mountains.

Archaeology and Architecture
With a well-positioned harbour, Portimão found favour with the Phoenicians, Greeks and Carthaginians, who left behind them various Dolmen passage tombs dated from between 3500BC and 3000BC at Alcalar. One or two of these are still in excellent condition. The Arabs were ousted from the town in 1250 by the Knights of the Order of Santiago at the same time as Silves was liberated.

The Parish Church was probably started in the 14th century, and has 17th- and 18th-century *azulejos*. Other churches in the area have 16th- and 17th-century features. The town hall and many houses in the centre of Portimão date from the 18th and 19th centuries.

Seats in the shaded square of Largo 1 de Dezembro feature blue and white *azulejos* which depict important dates in Portugal's

Left This traditional batik boat, one of several examples, is an incredible piece of specialist work. Batik, one of the oldest known crafts, is an ancient Far Eastern art, introduced to Europe by the Portuguese and Dutch in the 17th century.

Below The Alcalar burial chambers are Dolmen passage tombs which probably date back to 3500BC. Thirteen beehive-shaped chambers, most of which were in a dilapidated condition when excavated, are now in the process of being restored with one or two ready for viewing.

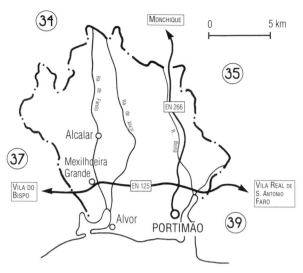

Fauna, Flora and Birdlife

The Alvor estuary is a very important breeding site for Black-winged Stilts, Kentish Plovers and a few Little Terns. Many waders, including Avocets, Spoonbills, Black- and Bar-tailed Godwits, Whimbrels and Grey Plovers, winter on the salt marshes, which are due to be designated as a nature reserve. Around here you can also see Waxbills, Dartford and Sardinian Warblers, Bee-eaters in summer, Bluethroats in autumn, and Stone Curlews on the more arid parts during winter. Shellfish are collected in the narrow estuary and a fish-farming unit operates near Mexilhoeira Grande.

In terms of plant life, the limestone area is rewarding, especially at Morgado de Arge, where in February magnificent examples of *Narcissus gaditanus* can be seen, as well as the Toothed Orchid and Paper-white Narcissus. Judas Trees and various species of mimosa line the roadsides to Monchique. The Australian Mimosas were originally brought over for the tannin contained in their bark.

Dragonflies and Damselflies are common during the summer – there are usually excellent opportunities for photographs of the Emperor Dragonfly as he patrols his territory. Lang's Short-tailed Blue and Cleopatra butterflies are seen early in the season, closely followed by Blue-spot Hairstreaks, Small Copper and Speckled Wood, along with a wide variety of other species during the summer.

history, ranging from the Treaty of Zamora on 5 October 1143 to the Proclamation of the Republic on 5 October 1910, exactly 747 years later to the day! These seats were made in 1930 and the tiles came from Sacavém in the Lisbon region.

Alvor Parish Church dates from the 16th century but was renovated in the 18th century, and has beautiful Manueline doorways. The Parish Church of Mexilhoeira Grande also has Manueline features.

Landscape and Crops

Three rivers flow into the sea from this *concelho*: the Arade, Boina and Farelo. Recently, pasture and grain have taken over from rice production in the alluvial basins. Fruit grows on the hillsides where the limestone rock has been cleared, leaving a deep *terra rosa* soil. Citrus fruits and peaches are the main crops, but vines are also cultivated where the soil is shallower. The Carboniferous slate hills to the north, leading into the Monchique foothills, are covered with Gum Cistus, but afforestation in recent years has seen the land also given over to Eucalyptus and pine.

The Mandrake has possibly more associated medieval myths than any other plant, due no doubt to the narcotic substances in its leaves. It is said to shriek when pulled from the ground as the fleshy roots are supposedly in the form of a human body!

Crafts and Local Produce

Maria da Luz Bolotinha and Margarida Maria Fogaça Cabrita both make attractive willow baskets filled with pretty porcelain flowers, while Maria Francisca Oliveira Sebastião from Alcalar makes fans decorated with dried flowers.

José Henrique Gonçalves Eliseu has been working with glass according to the 'Tiffany' technique for the last thirteen years – this began as a hobby which he learnt in Canada. The coloured glass is first cut (with a diamond), then trimmed with copper tape and soldered, after which various oxides are used to colour the tape natural, copper or black for the final effect.

Portimão's *artesanato* school has been going for eight years and is attended by young and old alike. In that time its original membership of fifteen has increased to over four hundred, here and in Ferragudo and Lagoa in the neighbouring *concelho* of Lagoa (39). Members come from all around the country, including a number of retired people who come down by train from Lisbon. Besides being a place to learn new crafts, the school is also a place for like-minded people to get together.

Most shoeing of horses and mules is 'cold' shoeing, done by a travelling blacksmith who carries a small anvil and sometimes arrives with everything boxed on the

Farriers throughout Europe are a rarity – a local travelling farrier is a friend indeed. Horses native to southern Europe have very much harder hooves than those in the north, probably due to the hard summer ground and the natural selection of stock over the centuries.

back of a motorbike. Most 'tools of the trade' are imported from Spain, apart from the shoes, which come from Braga in northern Portugal (or are made locally) and the nails (*cravos*) which have traditionally been imported from England, but which are now available locally. The paring of the hoof is extremely difficult work as horses hooves here are very hard.

It is interesting that not so long ago most farm work was done by oxen (or more often cows!). These also were shod and because a cow's hoof is cloven, their shoes were made in two parts.

39 LAGOA

The small *concelho* of Lagoa is bounded by Silves (35) to the north and east, Portimão (38) to the west, and the Atlantic to the south. The town of Lagoa lies at the crossroads of the roads to its famous Carvoeiro beach resort and Silves. The trans-Algarve EN125 also passes through.

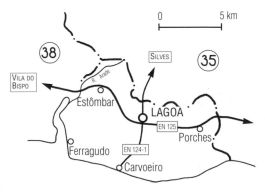

Archaeology and Architecture

This *concelho*, along with Estômbar in particular, had strong Arab connections and was the home of the famous Arabic poet Ibn Ammar.

The Parish Church is situated in an attractive square surrounded by Jacaranda Trees (with blue flowers during spring) and has a number of interesting features dating from the 13th century. The restored tower-belvedere of the one-time Convent of São José has distinctive grills over the windows and a *roda dos desprotegidos* (turn-box of the unprotected) on the ground floor which was for receiving foundling babies.

Estômbar's large church has three naves, Manueline external features and 18th-century *azulejos*, and occupies a prominent position at the top of the village. Ferragudo boasts the impressive 17th-century Fortaleza de São João, perched on high ground guarding the river estuary opposite its 16th-century Portimão counterpart, Fortaleza de Santa Catarina de Ribamar.

Landscape and Crops

The complex mixture of hard limestone and soft sandstone has been worn by the sea into dramatic cliffs and islands which are, unusually, colonized by large numbers of Cattle Egrets and a smaller number of Little Egrets. The extremities of the large bay stretching from Carvoeiro to Lagos are the only places in the world where this occurs, since as members of the heron family, they normally nest gregariously in trees.

This is now a demarcated area producing a predominance of red wine, and the fertile interior away from the urbanized coastline produces large quantities of grapes to supply the *adega* in Lagoa. Almonds, oranges, olives, figs and quince are grown between the vineyards, where you'll also find many hedges of Pomegranate bushes.

Fauna, Flora and Birdlife

Because of the exotic gardens of the villas and hotels along the coast there is an abundance of insects. Butterflies are numerous, and amongst the foliage you can usually find (or hear) an assortment of grasshoppers, crickets and locusts. Stick insects and praying mantis, either green or brown, are common and harmless, as are the large number of spiders which spin intricate webs amongst the bushes. Crab Spiders, which are usually white, lie in wait for prey in the centre of flowers. The only aggressive spider is the European Black Widow which can give a nasty bite but is not unduly dangerous and is only rarely seen. Many beetles are present, ranging from the huge Rhinoceros Beetle to the small but highly coloured Shield Beetle.

The Ribeira de Arade which forms the western edge of the *concelho* is in many areas highly vegetated, and has large expanses of mudflats exposed during low tide which are often covered with waders and gulls. Otters breed in the river banks in increasing numbers, and Mouse-eared and Lesser Horseshoe Bats can be found in the cave of Ibn Ammar.

The Naked Man Orchid is one of the most spectacular orchids found in southern Portugal. It is very local in distribution, but where it does grow it is prolific. It often grows in association with many other species, but always on limestone.

172

Crafts and Local Produce

Estômbar is known for its *empreita* work (palm basket weaving using dried Dwarf Palm leaves imported from Spain), which is still the finest in the area. The business was founded on 14 February 1916 and during the 1930s it employed 45 craftswomen. Now the numbers have dwindled and few still carry out this work, although others are learning. The Museu de Santo António in Lagos and another in Faro have examples of this fine work. Tiny hats and baskets are made here for the jute dolls at Martinlongo (13).

Estômbar is also the centre of production of elaborately decorated christening and wedding cakes.

In Pateiro, José António Vicente da Silva makes lovely miniature carts, replicas of ones which were used in bygone days, while in Ferragudo, José Rocha Cortes produces original sculptures and reliefs on unpolished marble.

Between 1920 and 1940 there were around 200 artisans in Lagoa involved in ceramic work, making it the area's most important industry. There are fewer still employed by the craft today, but the situation has recently changed for the better. With the help of the municipality and the cultural heritage institute, Fernando dos Santos Rodrigues, grandson and son of master potters, has opened the traditional pottery school of Lagoa, where he teaches secondary school pupils during the week and adults on Saturday.

The Adega de Lagoa is a cooperative cellar which has been making wine for the

Water carts like this miniature one with the earthenware containers were in use throughout the villages and more remote places until the advent of public standpipes or water being laid on to the individual cottages. Now they remain only as exhibits in ethnological museums!

Using local stone and marble one man makes sculptures in Ferragudo, mainly plaques. Ferragudo is a delightful small village which overlooks the Rio Arade and Portimão harbour, with a small castle protecting the entrance.

last 35 years. Today it produces about 45,000 hectolitres annually of *tinto* (red), *branco* (white) and *rosé* wines. Grapes are harvested in September and October, and then put into presses, after which the liquid is fermented for three months. Bottles are washed one day (automatically), filled the next, and then stopped with locally made corks and foil tops. The labels are stuck on by hand and the bottles manually packed into boxes.

Brandy is also produced here for sale privately or in specialist shops. The *adega's* prize exhibits are two barrels which hold 25,000 litres of 10-year-old wine, and a number of smaller barrels holding sweeter wine of the same age. The oak casks which hold these wines were made in northern Portugal.

40 ALBUFEIRA

Albufeira *concelho* is bounded by Silves (35) to the west, Loulé (41) to the east, Alte (18) and Benafim (19) to the north, and the Atlantic to the south. It is accessible by the recently completed IP1 motorway (known as the 'Via do Infante' in the Algarve) from north-west Portugal and Lisbon, which bypasses Albufeira *en route* to Seville in Spain. The original EN125 main coastal

Gulls are always voracious feeders and can usually be seen squabbling in harbours where fish are cleaned on the boats. It is interesting to check their identification as there can be unusual species around. These are Yellow-legged Gulls, close relatives of the Herring Gull.

road also runs through Albufeira. The town itself is still a working fishing village, but is now better known for its tourist attractions.

Archaeology and Architecture
The Romans, then the Visigoths and later the Arabs all inhabited Albufeira, with the Arabs finally being ousted by the Knights Templars in 1250 during the reign of Dom Afonso III. The old town's Misericórdia Chapel and Church of São Sebastião date from the 16th century and have Manueline doorways.

The remains of Paderne's ancient castle command magnificent views over the valley below, where an impressive Roman bridge crosses the river.

Landscape and Crops
Sandy beaches and ochre-coloured cliffs typify this coastline, helping to make it popular with tourists from throughout the world. Away from developed areas, the land rises gently in a mixture of sand and limestone hills, where traditional farming produces almonds, figs, olives, Carob Beans, Japanese Medlars, Pomegranates, quinces, apricots, peaches, oranges and lemons. In the red sandstone near the coast there are some magnificent stands of Umbrella Pine, with its distinctive heavy and rounded crown, which produces the pine kernels of commerce.

During spring many hundreds of hectares are covered with *favas*, broad beans which grow exceptionally well in this climate and mature early. These are mostly transported to Lisbon for canning.

Fauna, Flora and Birdlife
As you move further north in the *concelho*, the land becomes wilder; the highest point of 194m is at Malhão, just south of Paderne. Near the road at Boliqueime is the confluence of the Ribeira de Alte and Ribeira de Algibre, which together form the Ribeira de Quarteira, entering the sea at Vilamoura. Here the hillsides are covered in maquis scrub and the dominant shrubs of Kermes Oak, Gum Cistus and Mastic Tree, along with Winter Jasmine, Jerusalem Sage, two species of asphodel and Dwarf Fan Palm (the only native species of palm in Europe).

Although reptiles are present in quantity, there are not as many of them as you find in the Eastern Mediterranean. The Moorish Gecko is common and found near houses and ruins. As with all lizards and geckos, they are completely harmless – despite whatever folklore you may hear to the contrary. The most likely lizards to be seen are the Spiny-footed, Iberian Wall and the large green Ocellated Lizard. Snakes usually vanish quickly into the undergrowth, and the only venomous one is Lataste's Viper, but this is very rarely seen. The common ones are the Grass Snake, Viperine, Ladder and Horseshoe Whip Snakes, Southern Smooth and False Smooth Snakes, plus the huge Montpellier, which often grows to 2m.

The low land behind the sand dunes near Vale de Parra still holds a number of interesting birds. Little and Great-crested Grebes can be seen in the remaining water courses, while Black-winged Stilts breed amongst the rushes, and Kentish and Ringed Plovers can often be seen on the sand dunes.

Crafts and Local Produce
João Teodosio da Silva in Ferreiras is one of just a handful of cartwrights who still work along the coast. Carts are made from four different woods: the boss (hub) and wheel fellys (curved pieces of the circumference) from Ilex Oak; spokes from the Brazilian Mango Tree; the cart body from pine; and the shafts from Eucalyptus. The wheels have iron rims which form the outer protection. The rims are made to measure and are fitted by first heating over a very hot fire, hammering into place round the circumference and rapidly cooling with water from a watering can, thus contracting the iron around the fellys. Suspension is provided by leaf springs, which offer a little relief from bumpy terrain.

In the early part of the year vast areas of cultivated land shines yellow with the Bermuda Buttercup. Introduced as a garden plant from South Africa in the 19th century, it is a noxious weed which has spread to most Mediterranean areas.

Mule and donkey carts are now the exception rather than the rule. A quarter of a century ago they were used throughout the region. Some still exist along the coastal strip, although with difficulty, as many of the modern road systems prohibit their use. In the rural areas they are more common.

The mechanical saws and plane are now electrically driven, but, when first installed more than forty years ago, they were belt driven from the still present hand-turned cart-wheel which was geared to give the necessary speed.

The cart is painted with fine designs using a brush made from donkey hair (from the mane, since the tail is too thick) bound with cotton onto a toothpick.

41 LOULÉ

Loulé *concelho* is bordered by Faro (42) to the east, Albufeira (40) to the west, the Atlantic to the south, and Querença (25) and Benafim (19) to the north. The main town is situated on the EN270, which runs eastwards from Albufeira to São Brás de Alportel and Tavira. Only part of Loulé *concelho* is covered here since five of its *freguesias* were dealt with earlier.

Archaeology and Architecture
The Romans and Arabs both inhabited Loulé, the latter being evicted in the middle of the 13th century, and at Vilamoura there are the remains of a Roman villa.

The Gothic 13th-century Parish Church has three naves and decorative *azulejos* from the 18th century. In the centre of Loulé the walls of the 13th-century castle are impressive, although they are largely hidden from view. On a high point on the outskirts of the town, the circular 16th-century Chapel of Nossa Senhora da Piedade dominates the landscape.

Within the town is an unusual modern, imperfect-looking pillar, erected to the memory of a Minister of Works who was killed at a young age in a road accident in 1943.

Landscape and Crops

The land between the sea and the EN125 was, until a few years ago, heavily wooded with Umbrella Pine and scrubland, with marshland where the Ribeira de Quarteira and Ribeira de São Lourenço empty into the sea. Realizing the potential of this site, speculators developed Vilamoura and Quinta do Lago with sophisticated apartments, spacious villas with manicured gardens, and magnificent golf-courses, with the result that it has become a popular holiday resort.

Inland from the coast, the limestone hills rise to 362m near Loulé. At Loulé itself there is a rock-salt dome, which is being mined at a depth of 230m. Mined for the chemical industry, it yields mainly sodium-magnesium chloride which is coloured pink with mineral oxides.

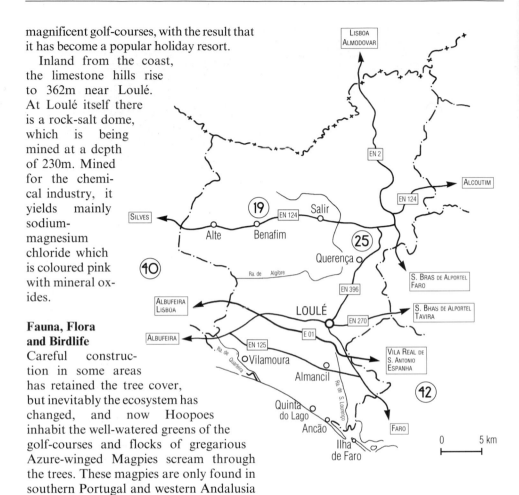

Fauna, Flora and Birdlife

Careful construction in some areas has retained the tree cover, but inevitably the ecosystem has changed, and now Hoopoes inhabit the well-watered greens of the golf-courses and flocks of gregarious Azure-winged Magpies scream through the trees. These magpies are only found in southern Portugal and western Andalusia in Spain and then in China and Japan. They are assumed to have been brought back by Portuguese sailors as cage birds during the 16th and 17th centuries and subsequently released.

In Quinta do Lago, 'Nature Trail' walks with hides provided have been developed with the aid of the Ria Formosa Nature Reserve so that rare birds can be seen. This has been so successful that the Purple Gallinule can now be observed with ease in the reed beds on the golf-courses.

Quinta do Ludo, a private property, forms an integral part of the Ria Formosa Reserve, and in winter from pathways outside you can often see flocks of Greater Flamingo and Spoonbills, along with hundreds of Shovelers, Mallard, Wigeon, Teal, Pintail, Pochard, Gadwall and in the fresh water river near Faro Island, Tufted Duck. Grey Phalarope have been seen spinning in the pools, and Ospreys can often be observed catching Grey Mullet from the lakes.

Where there is sufficient soil, almonds, olives, Carob Beans and figs are grown extensively for processing factories along the coast. Citrus fruits, peaches and apricots are grown in the many market gardens.

Above In many cottage court-yards in the villages maize and carob beans are spread out in the sun to dry. These will be used as feed for domestic livestock. This house, away from touristically orientated ones, has thick walls and no windows, keeping it cool in summer and warm in winter.

The Six-spot Burnet is a very attractive day-flying moth usually seen in mid-spring. It is notable in-so-much as it exudes cyanide as a defence mechanism, there-fore making it extremely distaste-ful to predators.

Crafts and Local Produce

Almancil has two artists: João Carlos Rodrigues, who works with stained glass, and his wife Maria Cristina, who paints silk to make attractive scarves.

Loulé is always considered to be one of the most craft-oriented towns in the Algarve. Many artisans here work with Dwarf Palm making baskets and mats, while the *Pedreira de Loulé* makes tables from locally quarried stone. Leather work in the form of belts, handbags and saddlery is made in the town, and Ilídio Marquês works with copper and brass in his workshop near the old town walls. Of the 30–40 coppersmiths who used to work in Loulé, he is the only one left.

Loulé's fame today stems partly from its colourful carnival at the beginning of Lent. With the advent of tourism, the weekly Saturday gypsy market has become something of a modern tradition.

Throughout the region Dwarf Fan Palm leaves are woven into baskets that are used for shopping, and seen in shops holding jewellery or the local marzipan cakes. They are also made into table or floor mats.

42 FARO

Faro *concelho* is bordered by Loulé (41) to the west, Olhão (43) to the east, the *freguesia* of São Brás de Alportel (26) to the north, and the Atlantic to the south. It is situated on the EN125, which joins the new IP1 Lisbon to Seville motorway.

Archaeology and Architecture
The town of Faro, situated about 150km from Cabo de São Vicente to the west and 50km from Vila Real de Santo António to the east, is the capital of the Algarve, and is bordered by a series of shallow sandy islands on its southern seaward side. It was a trading post for the Phoenicians and Greeks, before becoming Roman *Ossonoba*. Conquered by the Visigoths in 418, it was later over-run by the Arabs in 714, who in turn were overthrown in 1249. In 1540 it became a city and in 1577 it was declared the capital of this southern district of Portugal.

In 1596 it was sacked by the Earl of Essex, who took back to Queen Elizabeth I numerous books from the ecclesiastical library, which subsequently formed the basis of the collection at the Bodleian Library at Oxford. Napoleon's forces were expelled from here in 1808.

It is a city full of historical buildings, although due to the destruction by the Earl of Essex and the havoc caused by the 1755 earthquake, buildings constructed before that time were either destroyed or badly damaged. Their renovation has given a mixture of styles. Notable are vestiges of the 13th-century city walls with the castle gate (reconstructed in the 18th century) leading into the cathedral square and old part of the town. Here the Romanesque-Gothic cathedral, built in 1251, is on the site of a mosque which itself was on a Roman Temple. Only two of the original chapels remain; the rest are a mixture of Gothic architecture. The 16th-century one-time Convent de Nossa Senhora da Assunção with its original two-storey cloisters now houses the municipal archaeological museum, with displays including 3rd-century Roman mosaics and *azulejos* from the 15th century through to the present. The 17th-century Bishop's Palace contained multicoloured decorative *azulejos* panels.

Roman ruins at Milreu outside the town of Estói are well worth a visit, with mosaics and a basilica from the 4th century. Estói palace, built in the 18th

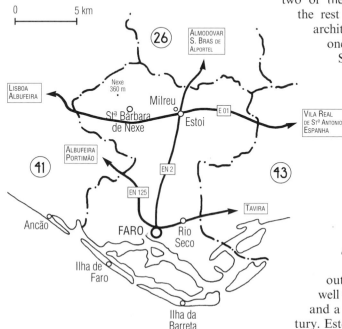

The palace of Estói is an extravaganza of mid-19th century art with some wonderful examples of *azulejos*. The depicted panel is of *Leda and the Swan* from classical mythology.

century and with later additions, has magnificent *azulejos* dating from the late 19th century. Also worth visiting in Estói is the 17th-century São Martinho church, renovated in the 19th century, and the Parish Church of Santa Bárbara de Nexe, which was originally built in the 15th century and has *azulejos* from the 17th century.

Landscape and Crops
This *concelho* is very similar to its neighbour, Olhão. The coastline lies entirely within the Ria Formosa reserve and in the main constitutes a series of sand spits and

islands. Both the Ilha de Faro and Ilha da Barreta are inhabited, but large areas are covered with water at high tide, providing feeding grounds for countless resident and migrant waders at low tide.

The fertile alluvial soil north of Faro is intensively cultivated with oranges, lemons, peaches and extensive vegetable crops, many of which are sheltered under plastic greenhouses during winter. The north of the *concelho* rises abruptly from the Faro plain in a series of steep limestone ridges, reaching a height of 360m at Nexe. The habitat here is very different, predominantly composed of almond, fig, Carob Bean and Olive trees, with an undergrowth of Mastic Tree, Kermes Oak and cistus species. There are also areas of pasture and, where the soil is deep, maize, grapes and cereals are grown.

Fauna, Flora and Birdlife
During spring this is one of the most beautiful parts of the Algarve. A large number of orchid species grow well in the limestone, including Bee Orchid, Yellow Bee, Bumble Bee, Woodcock, Mirror, Brown Bee (often called the Dull Orchid), Man, Naked Man and the Green-veined Orchid. The *Serapias* are represented by the Tongue and Heart-shaped Orchids, and the *Helleborines* by the Broad-leaved Helleborine.

The identification of most terrestrial orchids can present a number of difficulties, due to the fact that the family is still evolving. This means that closely related species can – and do – hybridize, leading to a wide variation in colour and form. One species which has stabilized its evolution is the Bumble Bee Orchid, all specimens of which are identical.

Irises colour the countryside in May, while the small Hoop Petticoat Narcissus and *Narcissus gaditanus* have to be searched for in the undergrowth. In winter the Paperwhite Narcissus is found in moist areas.

Cistanche phelypaea is an unmistakable and colourful parasite living on species of Chenopodiaceae and grows in restricted salt marsh areas between Cadiz in Spain and Cabo de São Vicente. The tall yellow flowers are dramatic and brighten the often drab landscape of the salt-marshes.

Crafts and Local Produce

To the east of Faro, on the main EN125 at Rio Seco, Joaquim António Boto is one of Portugal's last remaining coppersmiths. He has been in the trade for 45 years, during the past 20 of which he has been based in his present location, *Oficina de Cobres*, working with copper imported from Italy, Germany and Austria. He also works with aluminium and brass.

Starting with copper sheets, he cuts the metal to size, rolls it into a cylinder and solders it together. It is then heated over a furnace, before being plunged into ice-cold water and then beaten and moulded into shape on a work-bench. After each shaping, the heat and cold procedure is repeated as it makes the copper more malleable. After the final shape is acquired he hammers it to give it a traditional indented look. Many of the pieces are oxidized to give them an antique appearance.

Joaquim's showroom is full of attractive pieces, ranging from jugs and *cataplana* dishes (a cooking utensil a bit like a wok), to large ornamental buckets and fire guards. He will also make individual pieces to order.

Here the coppersmith is working on a *cataplana* dish in aluminium to fulfil an order. *Cataplana* dishes are closed pans similar to a wok, which are used to cook a variety of dishes, in particular a delicious seafood speciality that is typical of the region.

43 OLHÃO

Olhão is bounded by the Atlantic coast with its vast sandbanks to the south, Faro (42) to the west, and Tavira (44) to the east, and Santa Catarina da Fonte do Bispo (27) northwards. It is situated on the southern EN125 route, the EN398 to Santa Catarina da Fonte do Bispo via Moncarapacho, and the EN2-6, which joins the main EN2 at Estói.

Archaeology and Architecture

Olhão is a fascinating town and 'one of a kind'. The 18th-century fishermen's quarter has winding narrow streets and the low, square, flat-roofed houses (sometimes described as cubist) give it a Moroccan flavour. The *Jardim Pescador Olhanense* (Olhão Fishermen's Garden) which is near the market, is named to honour the 17 fishermen who sailed to Rio de Janeiro to tell the exiled Dom João VI of the departure of Napoleon's troops in 1808. These brave men followed Cabral's route to Brazil and went without charts or navigation aids.

Three of the many benches (seats) within the garden depict this great adventure with others showing traditional fishing scenes. The original tiles have been replaced by ones made in Aveiro in 1981–2.

The Parish Church in Moncarapacho has 17th-century *azulejos* and 18th-century paintings, while the Igreja do Santo Cristo

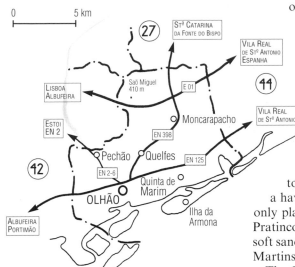

also has features from the same periods and is noted for its *Museu Paroquial* (Parochial Museum) containing religious art, archaeological and ethnological exhibits.

Landscape and Crops
The southern part of this *concelho* is an area of fertile alluvium, silt and sand often reclaimed from the marshland on the coast. Large areas devoted to intensive vegetable and fruit production are planted with early strawberries, sweet peppers, dwarf beans, cucumbers and tomatoes. Oranges, lemons and grapes are grown amongst the vegetables, but these give way to almonds, figs, olives and Carob Beans as the land rises further north, while maize, cereals and pasture land take over from intensive vegetable production.

A limestone ridge rising to 410m at São Miguel forms the northern edge of the *concelho*. This is a shoreline cliff from bygone ages and supports the typical *barrocal* vegetation of cistus scrub with an undergrowth

of orchids, narcissus, tulips, iris, scilla and a variety of annuals, as well as aromatic herbs such as thyme, lavender, rosemary and fennel.

Fauna, Flora and Birdlife
The coastline is all within the large Ria Formosa reserve, which protects the delicate flora and fauna of the 60km long salt marshes stretching from Quinta do Lago to Cacela-a-Velha. This area is also a haven for migrating birds, and is the only place in the Algarve where Collared Pratincoles nest. Where there are suitable soft sandstone banks, Bee-eaters and Sand Martins can be seen nesting.

The Quinta de Marim information and research centre (not to be confused with Castro Marim) is signposted from the EN125 on the eastern side of Olhão. Continue over the railway line after the campsite and it is well marked on the left.

The centre includes a conference area, offices for scientists, and demonstrations and exhibitions, including marine tanks, a large relief plan of the area showing outlying sandbanks, and a private collection of lamps and lanterns dating from Roman times. Further showcases are devoted to amphorae, fishing tackle, model boats and artefacts from recent excavations of Roman fish salting tanks.

The University of Algarve in Faro has a trial area studying soil erosion and rain conservation.

A bird recuperation centre with a large flight tunnel – one of only three in Portugal – recovers injured birds from shooting, oil slicks, exhaustion or any other mishap, treating and releasing them as soon as they are fit to fend for themselves again. Great importance is given to breeding the rare Algarve Water Dog. Equally important are conducted tours for children.

A useful map is available when you enter the centre, showing pathways and pin-pointing locations, including a picnic site. Notice boards explain the various features as you come to them.

Plants within the Umbrella Pine woodland include *Fritillaria lusitanica*, *Romulea bulbocodium*, Spanish Iris, *Gladiolus illyricus*, Grape Hyacinth and many more. The Mediterranean Chameleon also has a stronghold here.

Birdlife along the shoreline is very rewarding, with a variety of species seen according to the season. Curlew and Whimbrel, Kentish, Ringed and Grey Plover, Dunlins and Sanderlings, Oyster-catchers and Turnstones, Redshanks and Greenshanks, and Little Terns, which dive gracefully into the sea, are all here. On the salt marsh habitat the rare and striking *Cistanche phelypaea* grows; it is an elegant, yellow-flowered plant parasitic on Chenopodiaceae.

Inshore lagoons have nesting Black-winged Stilts, Yellow Wagtail (blue-headed form), Little Egrets and White Storks. Greater Flamingo often pass overhead and occasionally rest here. An inland lake overlooked by a hide is home to Little Grebes, Coot and Moorhen, with Great Reed Warblers and Bee-eaters nesting around the edge.

A five-month-old Algarve Water Dog. At first sight they look like a Poodle, but have membranes between their toes and were used on the fishing boats as working dogs. They can dive up to 6m deep! Note the typical pavement, *calçada,* which is made from limestone cubes.

Nearby are the landscaped archaeological discoveries of Roman sardine salting tanks, remains of old habitations, and lime kilns.

A renovated tidal mill has six large mill stones, some of which are original but with new hoppers and chutes. After the tide has entered the large holding lake, the sluice gates are closed. As the tide retreats, small exits to the sea are opened (one for each mill), and the water revolves the turbines which work the mechanism for grinding the grain between the stones.

Crafts and Local Produce

The Custódio brothers work in a small new factory area on the border of Quelfes, situated on the left just beyond the large cemetery as one travels from Olhão to Moncarapacho. Here they fashion beautiful carvings out of driftwood of all shapes and sizes, and include enormous pieces suitable for mantlepieces and overhead beams.

Maria Jocelia Cruz makes *azulejos* in her workshop, *Azulejos Aresta Viva,* at

The Pintail is a winter visitor to the Algarve having spent its breeding season in northern Scandinavia and Siberia. It is a distinctive surface-feeding duck. The drake has a diagnostic white stripe down the neck. In breeding plumage the male has an even longer pointed tail from which it gets its name.

189

This single *azulejo* tile is made in the traditional method with a raised surface. Many of the original tiles were made under Moroccan or Spanish influence, although Dutch artists did come to Portugal in the 16th century to assist with this new conception.

Pechão, using traditional Spanish–Arabic designs. Examples of her work can be seen in museums in Germany, Lisbon and Faro, and many pieces have been designed for stairways, swimming pools and terraces. She produces both individual tiles and panels in primarily maroon, blue and yellow.

She makes her tile forms (or moulds) with plaster of Paris to give her the desired raised designs. She rolls out prepared clay like pastry, presses it into the moulds, then turns out the shapes to dry in an airy, sunless location for one week in summer and up to three weeks in winter. Next they are baked in a furnace for around 30 hours – 10 to heat up,

10 at a temperature of 980°C, and 10 to cool down. The oven is not opened until the temperature falls below 100°C.

For panels she works in a similar way by rolling the clay between two boards and then cutting it, usually into 14cm squares.

The tiles are then painted, covered with powdered glass for glazing, and fired once again using the same process.

44 TAVIRA

Tavira *concelho* is bordered by the Atlantic to the south, Vila Real de Santo António (45) to the east, Odeleite (23), Vaqueiros (22) and Cachopo (21) to the north, and Santa Catarina da Fonte do Bispo (27) and Olhão (43) to the west. It is well situated on the EN125 and has easy access to the IP1 motorway.

Archaeology and Architecture

Tavira has a long history and is believed to have been inhabited as early as 2000BC. During the late 15th century Dom João II made it his home and in 1520 it was designated a city. It has a large number of historic buildings, many with Manueline features, including the chapel of the church of Santa Maria do Castelo, and a vault in the church of São José. Nossa Senhora das Ondas is also thought to have been built during the reign of Dom Manuel I. The

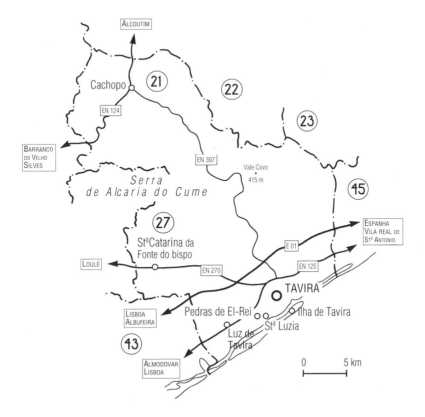

south door of the Parish Church in Luz de Tavira on the EN125 is generally regarded as being one of the most beautiful Manueline doors in the Algarve, showing many of the traditional features of the style.

Landscape and Crops
Away from the coastline are well-tended vineyards and orchards of oranges, lemons, figs and almonds. An olive grove near Pedras de El-Rei is reputed to be well over 1,000 years old and still produces fruit, with very old Carob Bean Trees there also of great economic importance.

North of the new trans-Algarve motorway (IP1) the terrain rises rapidly to the highest point in the *concelho* at Vale Covo (415m). Here the bedrock is hard slate which has been worn into high round-topped hills known as the Serra de Alcaria do Cume. This poor region is covered with cistus scrub, alleviated here and there with thin cereal fields and Eucalyptus plantations, while a few sheep and goats graze the grassland.

Fauna, Flora and Birdlife

The coastal strip here is part of the Parque Natural da Ria Formosa and comprises a lagoon complex and dune system known as the Ilha de Tavira, running parallel with the shore-line. Within this marshland are vast salt evaporation pans, the edges of which are used as nesting sites by Black-winged Stilts, Avocets and Little Terns. Many of the resultant chicks are 'ringed' by qualified ringers for scientific purposes. During the spring migration, exciting birds can easily be seen

The Little Tern is Europe's smallest tern. It has an elaborate courtship display during which the male offers his mate a Sand Eel while she is sitting on the ground near the nest prior to mating. The male often feeds the female while she is incubating the eggs or brooding the young.

The small fishing boats in the sheltered harbour of Santa Luzia, with one of the off-shore islands in the background. The earthenware pots are used for catching octopus and squid. They are roped together and after baiting are laid on the bottom of the shallow sea, where they attract their prey.

Huge heaps of salt are a familiar sight over the vast salt marshes in southern Portugal. In this case after evaporation and crystallization the salt is collected mechanically, but you can still see traditional, hand-collected heaps along the coastline.

from the road to the Ilha de Tavira. In May, Curlew Sandpiper (red and chestnut breeding plumage), and stunning Spotted Redshanks (black with white spotted breeding plumage) briefly stop to feed before flying on to their cold nesting grounds.

The marshland vegetation is colourful in summer, especially with the purple flowers of the Sea Lavender, and possibly the most astonishing plant is the *Cistanche phelypaea*, a rare but locally abundant parasite found on species of Chenopodiaceae. This strange plant has a large spike of brilliant yellow flowers 150cm high and is very like an *Antirrhinum* in form. Later in the year the Glasswort turns red, relieving the normally dull green of the marsh.

Mammals are present but rarely seen during the day. Reptiles and amphibians include Marsh Frogs and European Pond Terrapin, which are often found sunning themselves in freshwater rivers and ponds. The Iberian Wall, Spiny-footed and large green Ocellated Lizards hunt amongst the rocks and undergrowth, and can be observed closely if approached slowly.

Crafts and Local Produce
Salt production has been a Portuguese industry since Phoenician times, and many typical hand-worked small pans are still in use. Near Tavira, however, *Sopursal* has been using modern mechanical methods for 24 years on land which was typical *sapal* (salt marsh) marshland. Their annual production is 10,000 tonnes from 100ha, with the actual collection taking approximately ten days. The salt is pure and *Sopursal* produces 40–50 per cent of Portugal's entire consumption. They are the only Portuguese producers who use a similar system to that in the Camargue Salines du Midi in France, which are the most important salt pans in Europe.

The process is as follows: sea water is let into evaporating pans, and after evaporation more water is added. When the salt concentration reaches 25 Beaume the water is transferred to level, shallow pans until the concentration reaches a maximum of 28–29 Beaume, at which point crystallization takes place. The remaining water is then removed. If the concentration should go above 29 Beaume, the crystals would contain a high proportion of undesirable magnesium.

Salt is extracted mechanically from the pans by huge tractors and then transferred by conveyor belt to trailers, which carry it to enormous heaps. The salt is washed with cold water once before being transported to the factory in Olhão, where it is washed twice more before being ground into uniform crystals.

During summertime, rain can be harmful to the salt, but in winter a crust forms and the rain simply runs off. Working with salt, the machinery must be washed daily to minimize its corrosive effect, but even then maintenance costs are extremely high.

45 VILA REAL DE SANTO ANTÓNIO AND CASTRO MARIM

This most south-eastern *concelho* of Portugal is bounded by Tavira (44) to the west, Azinhal (24) to the north, the Rio Guadiana (forming the border with Spain) to the east, and the Atlantic Ocean to the south. It is very well situated on Portugal's southern EN125 and eastern EN122 routes, as well as being within easy access of the European E01.

Archaeology and Architecture
Vila Real de Santo António was built on the site of a previous village, Santo António de Arenilha, which was destroyed by the sea during the 16th and 17th centuries. In 1774 the Marquis of Pombal ordered the building of this rectangular planned town in five months, with all the streets radiating from the central black and white *calçada* (paved) square, Praça do Marquês de Pombal.

The village of Cacela-a-Velha was probably a Phoenician settlement, but there are also vestiges of the Roman occupation here. Its Parish Church, with three naves and 17th-century features, is beautifully situated overlooking the offshore islands and the ocean.

Castro Marim was inhabited in Neolithic times and the Phoenicians used it as a port. It was also important to the Romans, and in 1238 Dom Sancho II reclaimed it for the Christians. Its castle dates from the 13th century and is probably of Moorish origin. Included within its fortifications are the ruins of the Misericórdia Church and an ethnological and archaeological museum. The castle defences were greatly enlarged in the 17th century, only to be demolished by the 1755 earthquake. Nearby, the Fort of São Sebastião also dates from the 17th century.

Landscape and Crops

Vila Real de Santo António and Monte Gordo are both built on sand and marshland recovered from the sea at the Guadiana estuary. The south-western zone stretches along the coast to just past Vila Nova de Cacela and then back into the hills to Pomar, near to which is the highest point in these two *concelhos* at 187m.

The western part has a sand bank running parallel to the beach and joining the mainland near Manta Rota. This produces a quiet stretch of seawater bordered by sand dunes and salt marsh.

The Chameleon is normally seen clambering very slowly amongst shrubs or along tree branches, usually only going down to ground level to lay eggs. It can change colour but is normally a mixture of green and brown. The unusual eyes move independently, which gives a very strange appearance.

Following pages One of the last wooden fishing boats being made on the riverside. This is a fast-dying art now that so many of the modern boats are made from the lighter, moulded fibreglass. The one depicted is made from pine and is for the maker's own use.

Just back from the wooded coastline there is an area of intensive horticulture, where tomatoes, cucumbers and sweet peppers are grown.

Fauna, Flora and Birdlife
In the shallow lagoon in the western part, migrating birds flock to join the resident breeding birds, Sanderlings and Kentish Plovers scurry to and fro along the beach, and Little Egrets and Grey Herons stand motionless waiting for fish. Curlew and Whimbrel rest here before continuing their long journey, while the gregarious Black-tailed Godwits probe the mud with their long bills and, during the spring, Black-winged Stilts and Avocets scream at potential intruders from their nesting territory.

The extensive conifer wood at Monte Gordo has been designated a protected area as it is home to Portugal's largest population of Mediterranean Chameleon. This strange reptile is an endangered species, but its numbers are increasing due to the protection afforded here.

Small woods of Umbrella Pine are established on the sandy sedimentary coastline, with thyme, heathers and French Lavender forming dense undergrowth. Fruit orchards, vineyards and fields of maize and cereal predominate.

Butterflies are numerous around the fruit orchards away from the coastline, but on the coast the halophytic plant life of the salt marshland is not favoured by butterfly larvae.

The Reserva Natural do Sapal de Castro Marim e Vila Real de Santo António was decreed as such on 27 March 1975 and extends to 2,089ha. Castro Marim, gazing across the Guadiana to Spain, has an information and educational centre in the old castle at the north of the town. Most of the reserve is working salt evaporation pans and access is limited, but adequate observation can be obtained from the many roads which cross the area.

This is one of the most important wintering areas in Portugal for Spoonbills, Greater Flamingo, Avocets, Black-winged

The lagoons and sandbank seen from the old castle walls at Cacela-a-Velha. This is the eastern end of the Ria Formosa reserve which extends westwards for 50km past Faro to Ancão. It is a wintering and breeding ground for countless numbers of waders.

Stilts, and many hundreds of duck. During spring vast quantities of migrating birds rest here before moving north up the Guadiana Depression. Over a hundred White Storks can be seen resting on the farmland and marshland nearby, with another thirty pairs nesting in the Reserve, mainly in trees. Gulls are common, primarily Black-headed, Lesser Black-backed and Yellow-legged Gulls, plus a number of Mediterranean Gulls, which are distinguished from the Black-headed by their larger black cap and white wings. Many Sandwich Terns and several Little Terns can be seen nesting on the salt pan edges, and during winter Caspian Terns are usually spotted, unmistakable due to their much greater size and massive bright red bill. The Caspian is the world's largest tern and is similar in size to the Yellow-legged Gull.

Crafts and Local Produce

Several crafts are practised in these *concelhos*, including basket making out of various materials along the banks of the Guadiana river. Periodic courses are offered in Vila Real de Santo António teaching such crafts as the art of making traditional bobbin lace. One lady here also makes pictures in false enamel.

A number of boatyards are now operating, but with the advent of fibre glass and other modern products, traditional wooden boat building is becoming an art of the past. Equally, the European Union encourages the use of more up-to-date and more durable materials. However, it is still possible to see one or two diehard traditionalists continuing in the old fashioned way, making fishing boats for themselves out of pine.

GLOSSARY

adega	cellar	*Junta*	parish office
albarda	donkey saddle	*lingüiça*	seasoned smoked sausage
algodão	cotton		
amadia	top quality cork	*linha*	cotton thread
arrôba	15kg	*linho*	linen
artesão	artisan	*Manueline*	elaborate Gothic architecture from the time of Manuel I
azulejos	painted tiles		
barragem	reservoir or dam		
barrocal	type of limestone habitat	*mato*	thick scrubland between one and three metres high
batata doce	sweet potato	*medronho*	a spirit distilled from the Strawberry Tree
bifana	hot pork used as a sandwich		
bolo de mel	honey cake	*mó*	millstone
bolota	acorn	*molim*	mule collar
cadeira	chair	*nora*	water wheel using buckets on a continuous chain
cal	lime		
calçada	limestone paving		
caldeirão	cauldron	*ovo*	egg
cantoneiros	road builders	*paio*	seasoned smoked pork sausage
canudo	sleeve or tube		
charneca	scattered, low, often aromatic scrubland	*paposeco*	bread roll
		percebes	Goose Barnacles
chouriça	seasoned, smoked sausage with sweet pepper and garlic	*ponto*	stitch
		presunto	salted ham
		requeijão	curd cheese
concelho	council or borough	*rosmaninho*	French Lavender, usually referring to the honey
empreita	basketry with palm		
farmácia	chemist shop		
fava	broad bean	*sapal*	salt marsh
fios	threads	*serra*	mountain or hills
fonte	spring or source	*Sr.*	Mr.
freguesia	parish	*Sra.*	Mrs.
javali	Wild Boar	*taverna*	bar
		tesoura	scissors

BIBLIOGRAPHY

Afonso, M. da L.R. & McMurtrie, M. *Plantas do Algarve*, Serviço Nacional de Parques, Reservas e Conservação da Natureza, 1991

d'Aguilar, J. & Dommanger, J.L. *A Field Guide to the Dragonflies of Britain, Europe and North Africa*, Collins, 1986

Anderson, B. & Anderson, E. *Landscapes of Portugal, Algarve*, Sunflower Books, 1991

Arnold, E.N. & Burton, J.A. *A Field Guide to the Reptiles and Amphibians of Britain and Europe*, Collins, 1978

Blanchard, J.W. *Narcissus, a Guide to Wild Daffodils*, Alpine Garden Society, 1990

Buttler, K.P. *Field Guide to Orchids of Britain and Europe*, The Crowood Press, 1991

Carter, D.J. & Hargreaves, B. *A Field Guide to Caterpillars, Butterflies and Moths in Britain and Europe*, Collins, 1986

Chinery, M. *A Field Guide to the Insects of Britain and Northern Europe*, Collins, 1973

Condessa, M.B., Silva, J. & Garrido, J. *Algarve Portugal, Guide to Walks*, Algarve Tourist Board

Corbett, G. & Ovenden, D. *The Mammals of Britain and Europe*, Collins, 1980

Davies, P., Davies, J., & Huxley, A. *Wild Orchids of Britain and Europe*, The Hogarth Press, 1988

Finlayson, C. & Tomlinson, D. *Birds of Iberia*, Mirador Books, 1993

Heinzel, H., Fitter, R.S.R. & Parslow, J. *The Birds of Britain and Europe*, Collins, 1979

Higgins, L.G. & Riley, N.D. *A Field Guide to the Butterflies of Britain and Europe*, Collins, 1970

Humphries, C.J., Press, J.R. & Sutton, D.A. *The Hamlyn Guide to Trees of Britain and Europe*, Hamlyn, 1989

Jones, D. *A Guide to Spiders of Britain and Northern Europe*, Hamlyn, 1989

Mabberley, D.J. & Placito, P.J. *Algarve Plants and Landscape. Passing tradition and ecological change*, Oxford University Press, 1993

Polunin, O. & Huxley, A. *Flowers of the Mediterranean*, Chatto and Windus, 1990

Polunin, O. & Smythies, B.E. *Flowers of Southwest Europe*, Oxford University Press, 1988

Port, L. *Get to Know the Algarve*, Vista Iberica Publicações, 1993

Reichholf-Reihm, H. *Field Guide to Butterflies and Moths of Britain and Europe*, The Crowood Press, 1991

Vowles, G.A. & Vowles, R.S. *Breeding Birds of the Algarve*, Centro de Estudos Ornithológicos no Algarve, 1994

USEFUL ADDRESSES

Casa da Serra,
Empreendimento S. Luis Parque,
(near the municipal market)
FARO

Casa da Serra,
R. Antonio Pinto Castelar,
(near the police 'GNR' station)
SALIR

John and Madge Measures,
Quinta dos Almarjões,
Burgau,
8650 Vila do Bispo
Tel. 082 69152

All TURISMO Information Centres in the larger towns.

Associação "In Loco"
Rua Actor Nascimento Fernandes, 26-3
8000 FARO
Tel. 089-25032, fax. 089-27175

Parque Nacional Ria Formosa,
Quinta de Marim,
Quelfes,
8700 OLHÃO

For Travel Information:
The Travel Club of Upminster,
Station Road,
Upminster,
ESSEX RM14 2TT

INDEX